Slogans GALORE!

Gaelic words in English

George McLennan

NEW ARGYLL ✠ PUBLISHING

First published in 2010 by Argyll Publishing

This edition by New Argyll Publishing 2018

British Library Cataloguing-in-Publication Data.
A catalogue record for this book is available from the British Library.

ISBN 978-1-907165-32-0

CONTENTS

PREFACE

For most of the words in the word list below I have added a few remarks of a historical, grammatical etc nature. The following points, however, should be noted:

- I have not attempted to give any pronunciation guidelines for Gaelic words. Many other books and dictionaries deal with this, and readers who are interested may find *A Gaelic Alphabet[1]* helpful in this regard.

- I have given very brief explanations of features of Gaelic grammar such as lenition, eclipsis, spelling etc as they occur. Since the book deals with Gaelic words this is desirable for a fuller understanding of a particular word or point. Readers who want more information on these matters can consult any grammar book or language course, for instance *Scots Gaelic, an introduction to the basics[2]*. Indeed, I hope that readers who do not know much about Gaelic may be stimulated to have a closer look at this fascinating language. Features of Welsh grammar are also mentioned from time to time where they enhance the discussion of a Gaelic word.

- Many of the Gaelic words mentioned below also occur in some form or other in placenames and personal names. Since many readers will be quite familiar with these I've added examples where appropriate. The same goes for quotations from poetry (English and Scots) which may recall a half-forgotten word. Placenames are generally those of Scotland, but occasionally I've cited instances from England, as a reminder that a Celtic language was spoken all over England before it was gradually

---

[1] New Argyll Publishing ISBN 978-1-907165-34-4

[2] New Argyll Publishing ISBN 978-1-907165-36-8

ousted from the fifth century A.D. onwards by Anglo-Saxon and other later forms of English. I refer to this language, which was like early Welsh, as Old British.[3]

---

[3] This is a convenient term which, like Old Prussian, need not imply a later version of the language.

INTRODUCTION

For many reasons, including its status as a world language and because of its history as the language of the British Empire, the English language has been steadily enriched over the centuries by the inclusion of words from other languages. There are apparently words in English which have been borrowed from over 500 different languages throughout the world, from Aboriginal (e.g. *boomerang*) to Zulu (e.g. *impi*). Amongst these languages is Gaelic.

Gaelic words begin to appear in written English and Scots from the 9th century A.D. though they would presumably have been in circulation orally before this. They are found in ecclesiastical records, land documents and other official records. At that time there was no separate written Scottish Gaelic – or at least none has survived – but there was of course written Irish. Gaelic speakers in Scotland had come from Ireland in the 5th century, or perhaps even earlier. This written Irish was the form used in Scotland up to about the middle of the 17th century.[4] It is often referred to as Classical Irish, or Classical Common Gaelic, and all relevant borrowed words of this period are in the word list below. Since the same Gaelic was written in Scotland and Ireland it seems reasonable to include a word even if it has a strong Irish connection; it's still Gaelic and we can't assume that a word could be used in Ireland, but never in Scotland – or vice versa – during this period.

It is important to stress that it was the written language which was common to Ireland and Scotland. This did not apply to the spoken languages, and Scottish Gaelic gradually moved away from its Irish parent over the centuries and would have sounded quite alien to many Irish speakers by the 17th century. So for centuries

---

[4] There are occasional exceptions to this, such as the Book of the Dean of Lismore, which were written in a phonetic script based on Scots of the time. They throw much light on contemporary Scottish Gaelic pronunciation, but they do not concern us here.

there were two forms of Gaelic in Scotland, the learned written one and the unwritten vernacular, the latter finally gaining acceptance as a written language with the 1767 Gaelic translation of the New Testament, although alterations to the orthographic conventions have continued since then. It's rather like modern colloquial English compared with biblical English of the 17th century bible, the latter continuing in use in certain circumstances, but having vanished from everyday use. Other European languages provide parallels; there is quite a difference between colloquial spoken Welsh and standard written Welsh, the latter also biblical based. The best example is probably Greek, where the archaic *katharevousa* (pure) form of the language is still used in official documents. Modern Greek, known as *demotic* (popular), the everyday spoken language, has moved away considerably in grammar, vocabulary, and especially pronunciation from the *katharevousa* form, (although Greeks of today understandably tend to pronounce *katharevousa* following *demotic* speech).

A word borrowed into English may be described as Irish rather than Gaelic, but for reasons mentioned above I have included it in the word list. What I have not included are words from Irish which entered English from the later part of the 17th century to the present day, and which have obvious Irish associations, as *leprechaun* ('an elf') or *Dáil* (the Irish Parliament). Sometimes, however, a word from this period is described as Irish, but has the same form in Gaelic. An example would be **sluagh** 'a large number' (see under **slew**). Such words have been included.

The following have also been excluded:

a. old words belonging to the general Celtic language stratum, such as *druid* 'priest', *dun* 'hill', *sock* 'ploughshare', *brock* 'badger'; such words cannot be regarded as specifically Gaelic.

b. words which have a fortuitous similarity of sound to Gaelic but are otherwise unconnected. A frequently cited example is

4

smashin(g) which is thought to be from Gaelic **'s math sin** 'that's good'. In fact *smashin(g)* is from the verb *to smash* by way of extensions such as *smash hit, smasher* (of striking appearance) and has nothing to do with Gaelic **math**. The idea of vigour is also found in Scots where *smashing* means 'strapping, vigorous'. Compare the word *dashing* (striking, showy) from the verb *to dash*. Such folk etymologies are an occasional feature of languages and sometimes stick: Gaelic **buntàta** 'potato' is a compound based on the fortuitous fact that **bun** means 'root' and a potato is a root vegetable. Contrast the Irish *práta*. Sometimes, too, the fortuitous similarity between words in different languages can have the opposite effect, as Gaelic **na big** 'the *little*' (ones i.e. children).

Some readers may be surprised to find that words such as *tartan* are not in the word list. There are in fact quite a number of words with Highland / Gaelic associations which have nothing to do with Gaelic; dram, heather, Jacobite, kilt, peat, pibroch, skirl (of the pipes), mod and tartan are some which come to mind. Their origins are Greek (dram), English (heather), Latin (Jacobite, pibroch), Norse (kilt, skirl, mod) and Old British (peat), which provide a good illustration of the point made earlier about the enrichment of the English language. One could add here the name Dwelly, since Edward Dwelly was an Englishman, born and raised in England, who learnt Gaelic as an adult. His dictionary, mentioned below, remains a classic.

In compiling a list of words I have used Chambers English Dictionary (1992). If a word of Gaelic / Irish origin appears in Chambers I have included it, subject to the exclusions mentioned above. Chambers is a dictionary published in Scotland and so seems quite suitable for the present purpose. It may, of course, contain words which are not in other English dictionaries, particularly those marked (*Scot.*), and, conversely, other English dictionaries may contain words of Gaelic origin which are not in Chambers; North American dictionaries, for instance, may contain local words which are products of the Gaelic diaspora of the 18th and 19th centuries. And an Australasian lexicon should feature *barrow* 'to shear' (sheep) from **bearradh** 'shearing'. A dictionary of Scots also would contain a large number of additional words of Gaelic origin, and Sir Walter Scott had a fondness for using misspelt Gaelic words, as beal (**beul** 'mouth of a river' etc), bracken (**breacan** 'tartan') and brattach (**bratach** 'flag') to name but three. Dictionaries of a more specialised technical nature may also contain instances, as the relatively recent (1961) coinage *tacharanite*, a whitish mineral based on the word **tàcharan** 'ghost', 'changeling'. This mineral changes into other compounds when exposed to air, and is found on Skye (and elsewhere), hence this reference to its folklore. Piping also provides examples, not just the esoteric terms used in pibroch, but also the light music of marches, strathspeys and reels etc, which also feature the **taorluath** figuration, a term for which there is no English translation.

But a line has to be drawn somewhere and a word's entry in Chambers is the criterion. I have also made use of Dwelly's Gaelic-English Dictionary. This work is useful for identifying, by their absence, modern Irish words or forms. But things are not quite so simple. Dwelly used previous Gaelic dictionaries as the basis of his work (while of course adding a vast amount of new material) and since some of these earlier dictionaries contained words which were more Irish than Gaelic, these words duly appear in Dwelly. The author himself answers criticism of this by saying that such Irish words are in daily use in the Gaelic of Kintyre (**abair an dà latha**!) and appear in the Scottish Gaelic bible. Modern Gaelic dictionaries exclude most of them.

There are also words in the word list which go back to a non-Gaelic origin, but have a Gaelic form. So *pibroch*, mentioned above, is included, although it is ultimately from the Late Latin word *pipa*. The form *pibroch* relates to Gaelic **pìobaireachd** and was taken into English from Gaelic. The same can be said of *Hamish* in spite of its ultimate Hebrew origin. As this word indicates I have added names to the list, but again only if they appear in Chambers (in the section *Some first names*).

Most words in the word list are, not surprisingly, in English spelling, particularly placenames, as Argyll, Kilmarnock etc. But they are, of course, of Gaelic origin, and so have been included. I would also have included items from the section entitled *Phrases and quotations from Latin, Greek and modern foreign languages*, but there is no Gaelic there; there is just one Irish phrase − *Erin go bragh* 'Erin (Ireland) forever' (which leads one to wonder why **Alba gu bràth** isn't in, especially in Chambers) and one Welsh one − *pleidiol wyf i'm gwlad* 'loyal am I to my country', the phrase found round the edge of a Welsh pound coin. The Scottish pound coin has neither Gaelic nor English, but Latin *nemo me impune lacessit*, the motto of the Black Watch.

Finally, there are some occasions where authorities disagree on whether a word appeared first in Gaelic or in English (or Scots), and consequently which language influenced the other. Where such uncertainty exists I have mentioned it under the words concerned.

A

Abthane: Abbey lands, monastic territory. The modern word for an abbey is **abaid**, and mediaeval Irish had a form **apdaine**, with a hypothetical Gaelic form **abdhaine**. This was written *abthania* in Scottish mediaeval Latin because the **d** in early Irish was pronounced like a voiced **th** (as in then). This is not unusual; it's how **d** is pronounced today in Greek and, in most instances, in Spanish. The word for Gaelic itself, **Gàidhlig**, appears as *Gathelik* in early Gaelic (before the 13th century), reflecting a form *Gadelic* or similar when the **d** was unlenited.

The placename Appin in Argyll refers to Abbey lands connected with the nearby island of Lismore mentioned above; there was also an Appin in Perthshire. Other places with the same root are Balnaba in Wigtown, Balinaby in Islay and Fonab in Perthshire.

WORD LIST

These can be contrasted with Abbotsinch, the old name for Glasgow airport, which is very much an English form with Abbot coming first and with a possessive **s**. The Gaelic form would be **Innis an Aba**.

Mac an Aba is the Gaelic form of Macnab, the Perthshire clan whose chiefs are buried on an island in the River Dochart at Killin. It is also a fanciful name for the ring finger, otherwise known as **màthair na lùdaig**. A scurrilous saying about the MacNabs is:

> **Mac an Aba, sìol nan gaba,**
> **Cluasan fada is claigeann**
> **fèidh.**
> MacNabs, a clan of big mouths,
> Long ears and skulls of deer.

Aidan, Aiden: fire. A male forename, from Old Gaelic **aed**, later **aodh**, the latter form also now obsolete. It occurs also in the name Mackay, **MacAoidh**, where the final **d** has been lenited and so the sound disappears, as is normal in Gaelic. The ending **-an** is the sign of the diminutive in Gaelic masculine nouns, often used affectionately – 'little Aed'. The English word *ed*ifice is a cognate; its original meaning, from Latin, is a building with a hearth or fireplace. Aed or Aodh is the name of several early kings, and Aidan was also the name of a monk from Iona who became the Abbot of Lindisfarne in England. There was also a Celtic saint (one of dozens, some very obscure) called Aed, who is commemorated in several place names, notably Kilmodan in Glendaruel, Cowal. Kilmodan is *Cill mo Aedan*, 'Church of my Aedan'.

Airt, airth: direction, point of the compass. Gaelic **àird**.

Of a' the airts the wind can blaw
I dearly like the west,

wrote Burns at the start of his poem of the same title.

Aisling: a dream, a vision. Gaelic **aisling**. Also a female forename, usually Anglicised as *Ashling*.

Alasdair: defender of men, from Greek. A male forename, this is the Gaelic form of Alexander, also spelled Alastair, Alistair, and Alister, though the last two would not be correct Gaelic forms, and there is also a Mac surname based on these. The *-ander* part of Alexander, meaning 'man' is also found in the common Scottish name Andrew, 'manly'. Ailsa Craig, **Creag Ealasaid**, the large rock in the Firth of Clyde south of Arran has **Creag Alasdair** as one of its Gaelic names. There is also a Gortonallister in the south east of Arran, and Dunalister (formerly Murlaggan) between Lochs Tummel and Rannoch in Perthshire.

Angus: one choice. A male forename and surname. Gaelic **aon** 'one' and an obsolete root **gus**. The latter appears in Dwelly as an obsolete word one of whose meanings is 'wish, desire' See also under **Fergus**. The Gaelic form **Aonghas**, where the lenited **g** is not sounded gave rise to the now rather old-fashioned form (A)eneas – which, unlike French Énée, has no connection with the Trojan founder of Rome – and also to the surnames MacInnes, **MacAonghais**, and, probably, Neish.

The coastal lowland part of Angus is **Machair Aonghais**, (see under **machair**) while the Angus glens, including Glas Maol (see under **muley**) are **Bràigh Aonghais**. Angus was part of the Pictish kingdom, and was named after the 8th century king Angus or Oengus, son of Fergus, once the Scots had muscled in on Pictish territory. Previously it, along with the Mearns (see below under **mormaor**), had been known as Cirech or Circinn.

Argyll, **Argyle**: coastland of the Gaels. Gaelic **Earra-Ghàidheal**. Gaels came across to Argyll from the north of Ireland from around the 4th and 5th centuries A.D.

The word is also used to mean 1) a type of gravy boat intended to keep gravy hot (a design of the 4th Duke of Argyll), 2) a diamond-shaped pattern on socks loosely based on a Campbell tartan, and 3) a motor car of the Argyll Motor Company, based mostly in Alexandria (a town not in Argyll), which ceased production in 1928.

Atholl: new Ireland. Gaelic **Athall**, from **ath** 'next' and **Fòtla**, an old poetic word for Ireland named after an ancient Irish goddess.[5] The **f** is lenited and disappears, in line with normal Gaelic practice. So here we have an instance of colonists using a name from their old country. Other old names for Ireland appear in place names in Scotland – Dalriada is perhaps the best known – just as this country has reused its names elsewhere in former colonies; so Scotland appears in Nova Scotia, and many towns are also reproduced (Glasgow / Glasco appears over 20 times in the

---

[5] Another old poetic word for Ireland, with which readers may be familiar, is **fáil**, since it appears in the name of one of the political parties in Ireland, **Fianna Fáil** 'Warriors of Ireland'.

USA alone) and Scottish surnames are given to many topographical features world-wide.

Atholl brose is a deluxe version of crowdie (raw oatmeal mixed with water), with whisky and honey added, refined enough to be drunk by Queen Victoria during her visit to Blair Atholl in 1844. (See also under **drammock**.)

B

Balmoral: of uncertain meaning. Gaelic **Baile Mhoireil** or **Both Mhoireil** (**baile** is a village or township, **both** is a hut.). Balmoral describes 1) a flat brimless bonnet usually of blue wool (also called a blue-bonnet), see also **Kilmarnock**, 2) a laced boot, and 3) a woollen petticoat. Balmorality is a jocular reference to Victorian decorum linked to an excessive enthusiasm for tartans and other superficialities as 'acceptable' Scottishness.

Banshee: a female fairy. Gaelic **ban-sìth, bean-shìth. Bean** is *woman* and is frequently prefixed, usually in the form **ban**, to nouns to give a female equivalent. So **banrigh** is a queen, **banaltram** is a (female) nurse, and so on. The wail of a banshee was thought to portend disaster. **Sìthean**, a fairy knoll, was where they lived, and the word features in place names such as Schiehallion, **Sìth Chailleann,** 'Fairy hill of the Caledonians'. Dunkeld, **Dùn Chailleann** and Rohallion, **Ràth Chailleann**, both meaning 'Fort of the Caledonians' are also in Perthshire. Other instances are Glen Shee, Shian Ferry at Loch Creran, Argyll, and Strontian, for which last see below.

Bard: a poet. Gaelic **bàrd**. From **bàrd** comes the surname Baird, and also Ward (of Irish origin), the latter from **mac a' bhàird** with the lenited **b** pronounced like a **w** in Irish Gaelic dialect (and also sometimes in provincial Scottish Gaelic, hence, for instance, Lawers for **Labhar** by Loch Tay in Perthshire).[6]

The word is also found in several placenames, as Tullybardine in Perthshire and, in the lenited form, Garyvard in Lewis and Monzievaird in Perthshire.

Robert Burns has his muse address him as 'my own inspirèd bard' in *The Vision*. Bards ranged from learned products of bardic schools writing in complex metres to humbler village bards (**bàird baile**) composing on local issues in a light-hearted way. They all had a certain status. A Gaelic proverb describes their three privileges:

Trì subhailcean a' bhàird:
Fios fithich gu ròic,
Cuireadh fial gu tàthadh
rann,
Tart mòr gu òl a dhram.
Three privileges of the bard:

---

[6] This is not, of course, to be confused with the English surname Ward, 'guard' (with which it is cognate). There is also an obsolete Gaelic **bàrd** meaning 'dyke, fence' and this may account for some instances of Baird, echoing English surnames like March, and sometimes, Wall.

A raven's knowledge of a feast,
A liberal invitation to assemble verses,
A great thirst to drink his dram.

Barp: a cairn, barrow. Gaelic **barpa**. In the Hebrides the word describes a chambered cairn of the 3rd millennium B.C. used for burials, with a passageway leading to the internal burial chamber, all covered with a mound of stones. Barpa Langass (Gaelic **Langais**) in North Uist is a fine example.

Bawn: an enclosure for cattle; a fortification. Gaelic **bàbhan**, from **bò** and **dùn**. Other forms, **bàdhan** and **bàghan**, are used in Sutherland to mean 'churchyard', usually enclosed, the spelling of the former being nearer to the Gaelic root.

Beltane: an old Celtic festival which took place on May Day, the first of May, or sometimes on other days at the beginning of the month. Gaelic **Bealltainn**, also commonly referred to as **Latha buidhe Bealltainn**. The root of the word is old Gaelic *bel* 'bright, white' and, probably, some form of **teine** 'fire', and appears in Tullybelton, **Tulach Bhealtainn** (Beltane hillock) a few miles north of Perth.

A bale – various spellings – (fire) is a bonfire, or beacon fire, and the word also appears in the Slavonic languages; *Belo*russia or *Bel*arus used to be called White Russia, and *bel*uga is the white whale. **Teine** is found in Achateny, **Ach(adh) an Teine** and possible Ardentinny, **Àird an Teine**, both in Argyll.

At Beltane fires were lit on hills and cattle were driven between them for purposes of purification. An old Gaelic saying **eadar dà theine Bhealltainn** 'between two Beltane fires' was used to describe someone in a critical dilemma, and also referred to the time of the year for sowing.

Ben: a mountain. Gaelic **beinn**. This is the general word for a mountain, but there are many others, as the well-known ditty (of which there are several different versions) points out:

In England a mountain's a mountain but when
The climber's in Scotland it may be a ben
A creag or a meall, a spidean, a sgor,
A carn or a monadh, a stuc or a torr.

So, perhaps not surprisingly, of the 283 (at the last count) Munros (see under **Munro** below) only 62 contain the word ben or **beinn**, and some of these, in their English form, are rather hidden from readers without Gaelic, as Blaven, **Blàbheinn** in Skye. For **creag** and **càrn** see below under **craig** and **cairn**.

Birlinn: a galley. Gaelic **birlinn**. These Hebridean ships had eight or more oars on both sides and a mast with a rectangular sail, and are depicted on various tombstones in the islands, as well as on the Arms of several clans. The word is of Norse origin, like so many Gaelic nautical terms. **Birlinn Chlann Raghnaill** is a famous poem of considerable length (566 lines, one of the longest Gaelic poems) by the 18th century poet

Alexander MacDonald, **Alasdair MacMhaistir Alasdair**. **Birlinn** occurs in a few placenames, as Port na Birlinne on Loch Scridain in the Ross of Mull, and Innis na Birlinn, with nearby **sròn** and **druim**, near Onich, a few miles south of Fort William; the last two are thought to resemble in some way the prow of a galley.

Bodach: an old man. Gaelic **bodach**. The root of the word is **bod** 'penis', and the Old Man of Storr, a pinnacle in Staffin, Skye was formerly **Bod Storr**, because of its phallic shape, until Victorian reticence changed it to **Bodach Storr**. (**Bod** and **bodach** are related, of course). *Old man* is used elsewhere of such structures, as *The Old Man of Hoy* in Orkney (where there was never any Gaelic) and *The Old Man of Stoer* in Assynt. It is also found in England e.g. *The Old Man of Conniston*, though this is not a stack. Bolnabodach, **Buaile nam Bodach** 'the old men's sheep fold' occurs in Barra, but Rhubodach, the ferry terminal in Bute is more likely to refer to **Bòd**, 'Bute'. In Scots the word

was used, in the form *boddoch*, to mean a mutchkin, a measure of liquid or powder.

Bog: a swamp, marshy ground. Gaelic **bog**. The Gaelic word is an adjective meaning 'soft', 'limp'; the word for a swamp is **boglach**. **Bog** is cognate with English *bow* in the meanings *weapon* and *bend* (one's head, body) with the general sense of yielding, giving way. A modern use of **bog** is to describe a paperback book, such as this one, as opposed to **cruaidh** 'hardback'. Given the nature of much of the terrain of this country it is not surprising that there are several place names with **bog**; Ladybank, **Leathad Bog** 'boggy slope' in Fife is probably the best known.

Bothan: a hut, an unofficial pub in Lewis. Gaelic **bothan**, from which, probably, comes English *bothy*, though the **th** sound in English is not a Gaelic sound. The word is of Norse origin, related to English *booth*. An old Gaelic form was **both**, now **bùth** (generally meaning 'shop'), and the *-an* ending is the diminutive indicator attached to masculine nouns. For an example of the -*ag* feminine diminutive see **rolag** below.

The surnames Booth and the Scottish form Boath are from this word, the latter also a place in Angus. Other well-known **both** placenames are Boleskine, Bohuntine and Bohenie, all in Inverness-shire, as well as Buchanan, **Both a' Chanain** 'The Canon's Hut', which is also a surname.

Brat: a cloak, mantle, cover. Gaelic **brat**. This word appears also in Welsh and Old English (which borrowed it from Welsh) and so it is really an old Celtic word. A modern usage is **brat-ùrlair** 'a carpet' (floor covering), and common also is **bratach** 'a flag'. **A' Bhratach Shìth** is the famous fairy flag of the MacLeods, on view in Dunvegan Castle. (See also under **Banshee**, above).

Brochan: porridge, gruel. Gaelic **brochan**. The word is cognate with English *broth* and *brew*. In the north east brochan is a cereal mixture fed to calves. According to an Uist proverb uncooked porridge is what makes a man of you:

Brochan reamhar amh do na balaich Is brochan tana bruich do na h-ighnean.

Porridge thick and raw for the boys And porridge thin and cooked for the girls.

Brochan in place names apparently meant *sludgy*, i.e. terrain of porridge-like consistency; so Drumbrochan, near Cumnock.

Brogue: a sturdy laced shoe. Gaelic **bròg**. Ultimately from Norse *brok*, appearing in old English as *broce*, plural *brec*, which became *breeches*, Scots *breeks*. As this suggests, *brok* was used for leggings and foot coverings combined, and brogue was used in this sense in earlier English (17th and 18th centuries). Shakespeare mentions 'clouted (i.e. with nails) brogues' in Cymbeline. Brogue is also used to mean a type of accented English, especially that spoken in Ireland. The origin of this meaning is not certain, but it is thought that it may relate to brogue as a shoe, a slightly derogatory reference to the Irish peasantry of earlier centuries with their basic footwear. This would presumably have arisen from visits to partly English-speaking (to some extent) towns, when the peasantry would have worn footwear and have spoken in heavily accented English. In the countryside they would have gone barefoot and have spoken Irish. French *sabot* 'clog' was used in the same way. Compare *clodhopper* – a type of heavy shoe or boot, and a clumsy rustic, a lout. This is the other way round, the word being first used to mean a lout, then a ploughman's shoe. Similar is the use of hobnails to describe rustics.

It is interesting to note that a connection between clothing and speech is also found in *flannel*. This word is from Welsh *gwlân* 'wool' (a lenited or mutated **g** in Welsh disappears). In Shakespeare's 'The Merry Wives of Windsor' Falstaff describes a Welsh minister's words as 'Welsh flannel'.

Bealach nam Bròg, the site of a battle of uncertain date (any time from 1300 to c. 1450) is about 10 miles north-west of Dingwall. The reason for mentioning shoes is unclear.

Bun: a dry stalk; a hare's tail. Gaelic **bun**. In Gaelic the word means *root*, *bottom*, and is common in placenames to signify the mouth of a river. So Bonawe, **Bun Abha** 'the mouth of the River Awe' in Argyll, and Bunnahabhainn, **Bun na h-Abhainne** 'the mouth of the river', the name of a famous distillery in Islay. A modern usage is **bun-sgoil** 'primary school'.

Buss: a kiss, smack. Gaelic **bus** 'mouth', which gives Scots *buss*, also 'mouth'. The slang variant *puss* (to rhyme with English *bus*) means 'mouth', 'face'.

C

Caber: a long pole made from a tree trunk, tossed by athletes at Highland games. Gaelic **cabar** 'a pole', 'rafter', 'deer's antlers'. A caber can be up to nearly 20 feet long and weigh about 130 lbs.

The difference in spelling and pronunciation of the English and Gaelic forms illustrate typical features of the two languages. The spelling and the pronunciation are connected, of course. The English pronunciation *caber* (with the **a** as in *paper*) is a result of the following **e** and the fact that there is only one **b**; *cabber*, following English spelling conventions, would have given a sound closer to the Gaelic. This doesn't happen in Gaelic because a double **b** isn't allowed.[7] The word is spelled *caber* in English because *-er* is a common English suffix; *-ar* is used only with words of classical origin (*cellar, grammar* etc); this is what lies behind the variant spellings as burs**a**r and purs**e**r, Mill**a**r and Mill**e**r etc. So English has changed the Gaelic spelling, and hence the pronunciation,

to fit in with its spelling conventions. This is fairly widespread with words from Gaelic, as Tob**e**rmory (Gaelic **Tobar Mhoire** 'Mary's Well'), Kam**e**s (Gaelic **Camas** 'Bay') and so on. It also happens with words from other languages, as English *Naples*, Italian *Napoli*, English *The Hague*, Dutch *Den Haag*.

Cabar fèidh: 'deer's antlers' was a war cry and the name of the pipe tune of clan Mackenzie.

Cabar can also mean a horn, and the word is related to Latin *caper* 'goat' (English *cap*ricorn). Gaelic follows Latin in linking it to rafters; Latin *capreoli* were timber props, like goat horns, and the French *chevron* (from Latin-derived *chèvre* 'goat') illustrates the same feature.

Cabar features in several placenames, as Cabrach at the south end of Jura and Gartincaber, some five miles west of Dunblane in Perthshire.

Caboc: a cream cheese covered in oatmeal. Also kebbock, kebbuck. Gaelic **càbog**,

---

[7] Nor is a double p, which explains the spelling of Apainn, (mentioned above under **abthane**). English wants to keep the a (as in *hat*) sound because of related words *abbot, abbey* etc and so has to spell the word with a double p (Appin).

càbag 'a cheese'. This word is not really used nowadays (**mulchag** is used instead), but **ceabag** appears in Dwelly (from an informant in the Kyle of Lochalsh), probably from **ceap**, the wooden wheel of a barrow. **Càbog** appears to be a form of this, possibly influenced by Scots *cabok* (various spellings), but the stressed long vowel of the Gaelic (indicated by the accent) seems at odds with this. Normally an English short vowel would have no accent when borrowed into Gaelic, as **banca**, 'bank'. Culcabock **Cùil na Càbaig** just outside Inverness appears to mean 'cheese nook', but this seems odd and there are other explanations.

Cailleach: an old woman. Also caillach, cailliach. Gaelic **cailleach** 'old woman', 'a nun.' The root of the word is the obsolete Gaelic **caille** 'a veil, hood', which is the Q-Celtic[8] version of Latin (and

English) *pallium* 'a cloak', from which comes English *pall*. Nunton in Benbecula is **Baile nan Cailleach**. Caliach Point, **Rubha na Caillich** on the north-west of Mull, was named after a rock shaped like the head of a woman, and there is another **Rubha na Caillich** on the south-east of Jura.

Cain: an old Scots legal term referring to rent paid in kind, usually fowls or other livestock. Also kain. Gaelic **càin**, 'a tax', 'rent', 'tribute', 'fine', the last being the most common meaning today. Scots legal documents contain many references to *cain / kain-hen, -wedder* etc, and the phrase *pay the cain*, meant *pay the penalty*. This is thought to be one of these words (around 300 of them) taken into Gaelic from Latin, since the Latin word *canon* was used in the Roman empire to mean an annual tribute paid in kind (grain etc), though there are difficulties with this, and there are other derivations of **càin**.

Caird: a tinker, vagrant. Gaelic **ceàrd** 'a tinker', 'smith';

---

[8] Q-Celtic languages (Gaelic, Irish, Manx) generally have c where P-Celtic languages (Welsh, Breton) have p. Welsh has *pall* 'a pall, mantle'.

ceàrdach is a smithy. The surname Caird is from this word, as are several placenames, as Balnaguard, **Baile nan Ceàrd** 'Settlement of the Tinkers', and Dalnacardoch, **Dail na Ceàrdaich** 'Meadow of the Smithy' both in Perthshire. A well-known tinkers' name was Stewart, and there is a saying

Fuil nan Stiùbhartach anns na rìghrean is anns na ceàird

The blood of the Stewarts is in kings and in tinkers.

As James V observed, not all Stewarts were related to the king, and many clansmen had the same name as their chief, but were otherwise quite unconnected with him.

Cairn: a conical heap of loose stones erected as a memorial or landmark; more formal examples may use cement. Gaelic **càrn**, which can also mean a hill, as the lines quoted under **ben** above show. The word is related to **carraig** 'a rock' (see below under **crag**) and has the basic meaning 'hard'. There are dozens of placenames from

càrn; Cairnbaan, **An Càrn Bàn** 'The white cairn' by the Crinan Canal in Argyll and Lochcarnan, **Loch a' Chàrnain** 'Loch of the small cairn' in South Uist are two of the better known. In the sense of 'hill' the word appears in several Munros; Cairngorm, **An Càrn Gorm** 'the blue-green hill' is the most famous. Byron, in his poem Don Juan, describes the hero's 'brilliant breeches bright as Cairn Gorme', though the cairngorm gemstone is generally dark amber in colour. The surname Cairn(s) is also from this word, originally signifying someone who lived near a **càrn**.

The phrase **cuiridh mi clach air do chàrn**, 'I'll put a stone on your cairn' is used as a way of denoting friendship and affection for someone, from the habit of adding a stone to a cairn as a mark of respect.

Caman: a shinty stick. Gaelic **caman**. **Camanachd** is 'shinty', also known as **iomain**; *camogie* is the name in Ireland for hurling (a game similar to shinty) played by women. Unlike *caber* above,

caman retains its Gaelic spelling when used in English, probably because the word was not sufficiently well-known in Anglophone circles. *Caber*, on the other hand, has long featured in events attended by royalty from Queen Victoria onward, and the word and its connotations are a good example of *Balmorality* mentioned above.

The root of **caman** is **cam** 'bent, curved, crooked', a word of general Celtic origin, found in Welsh, Breton etc, and probably appears in Scots *camshachle* and *camsheugh*, both meaning 'bent', 'crooked'. It occurs several times in Shakespeare, both in its main sense *awry*, and in its secondary meaning 'blind in one eye', or 'cross-eyed, squinting'; in Henry V, the Welshman Daffyd ap Llewelyn is referred to as Daffyd Gam[9] 'squinting', (or 'one-eyed') David'.

Cam meaning 'with a bend' is the also the root of **camas** 'a bay' which occurs in lots of placenames, as Camasnacroise in Morvern. It also features in the names Cameron and Campbell, discussed next.

Cam 'crooked' is also found in placenames in England, both in its Celtic form, as Cambridge, Cambourne etc, and in its English form as Hamble, Hambledon etc, from where it was imported into Lanarkshire as Hamilton *Hamel Dun* 'Crooked Hill'.

It is normal for Indo-European roots beginning with **k** to emerge in Gaelic beginning with a **c**, but in English beginning with an **h**, so that the English word *ham*, for instance, originally referred to the <u>bent</u> (**cam**) part of the leg behind the knee. Some common Gaelic examples are **cas** 'precipitous', 'rapid' / English *haste*; **còrn** 'drinking horn' / English *horn*; **coin** 'dogs' / English *hound*; **cuileann** 'holly' / English *holly*; **cumha** 'lament' / English *hum*.

Cameron: bent nose. A surname and a male forename. Gaelic **Camshron**. This is the traditional explanation, from **cam** 'crooked, curved' men-

---

tioned above, and **sròn** 'nose'. For **sròn** in place names see under **Strontian** below. There are, however, places in Fife, Edinburgh area and Lennox where the placename Cameron occurs, all well away from the clan's Lochaber heartland. The Fife Cameron in particular features frequently in old records, often spelled Cambrun or similar, so this may be the origin of the name, with the traditional explanation being a bit of folk etymology. The adjective Cameronian describes 1. a member of the Reformed Presbyterian Church, a very small remnant of which possibly still exists, and 2. a member of what later became the First Battalion of Scottish Rifles, no longer in existence.

Campbellite: a member of an obscure Presbyterian sect founded in the 19th century. The name Campbell features the word **cam** 'bent, crooked', and **beul** 'mouth'. The implication is that this was a striking facial feature of the clan founder, previously known as Ó Duibhne. It has also been suggested rather unkindly by those not well disposed towards the Campbells that the reference may also be metaphorical (of twisted speech). The insertion of the **p** in the English form Campbell is a relic of fanciful etymologising (*campo bello*) in the middle ages and shouldn't really be there. Compare also **ptarmigan**, below.

For **beul** see also under **port** below.

Canna: bog cotton, mountain down. Also cannach. Gaelic **canach**. This was apparently used to make garments, and some, woven by women from crofts in Inverness-shire and Ross and Cromarty, were exhibited at the Great Exhibition of 1851 in the Crystal Palace, London. The word means 'white', and is related to the English / Latin term *canities* 'whiteness of the hair'. Gaelic also has the word **càin** 'white' from the same Latin root. Bog cotton is widespread throughout the damp areas of the Highlands, and features in Cannich in Strath Glass and Urchany, just south of Nairn. In *The Lady of the Lake* Sir

Walter Scott describes the breathless silence of the lake 'still as the canna's hoary beard'.

Capercaillie: a large type of grouse, a wood grouse. Also capercailȝie, a spelling which features the old Scots letter *yogh* found also in the surnames MacKenzie and Menzies. Gaelic **capall-coille** 'horse of (the) wood'. This use of *horse* could be compared with hippocampus 'sea horse' – quite a small fish – and hippopotamus 'river horse', for which Dwelly gives the Gaelic **capall-abhainn**, a literal translation of the Greek. **Capall** is related to the English *cavalry* and other Romance language words, and appears in Capel Mounth, the track over the Grampians and, probably, in Capeldre in Fife. **Coille** is found in dozens of placenames; perhaps the best known is Killiecrankie in Perthshire, and Aucholzie, **Ach(adh) Choille** in Aberdeenshire, worth a mention because of its use of *yogh* referred to above.

Carfuffle: a mess, upheaval. Also curfuffle, kerfuffle. The first part of this word is thought to be the Gaelic adverb **car** 'rather, somewhat'. In Gaelic it is used only with adjectives, as in Scots *carnaptious* 'snappy, argumentative, irritable', but it also occurs in Scots with a verb, as *carmudgel* 'to damage', 'knock about', and **carfuffle** is also used as a verb.

Caschrom: a sort of foot plough, like an ice-hockey stick with a peg in the heel to put your foot on. Gaelic **cas chrom** 'bent leg'. **Crom** appears in several placenames; Cromarty and (Aber)crombie in Fife are probably the best known, the latter also a surname. See also under **crombie** and **cromack** below. Compare also **loy** below.

Cateran: a marauding brigand, a reiver. Gaelic **ceatharna** 'a marauding troop', though the **t** would not have a sound in the Gaelic.[10] The word is singular

---

[10] This sometimes happens with dentals (d and t). The **d** is retained in, for instance, Pitmedden 'middle farm' in

in English, but collective in Gaelic. It is probably related to English *quatrain* (more specifically Latin / English *quaternio* 'a group of four (soldiers)'), but a connection with Latin *caterva* 'a band of troops' is also possible.

Loch Katrine in the Trossachs is generally assumed to mean 'Loch of the Caterans'. This is the loch which features in Sir Walter Scott's poem 'The Lady of the Lake' (see below under **loch**), and on which the steamship *Sir Walter Scott* has been sailing for over a century (with breaks for restorations).

Catriona: The Gaelic form of Catherine, of uncertain meaning, though it may have a connection with Greek *katharos* 'pure' mentioned in the introduction. Gaelic **Catrìona**. A female forename. The accent on the Gaelic form indicates where the stress goes, i.e. it's not in its usual place on the first syllable

in a Gaelic word. So the Gaelic version is like the Italian, Spanish etc pronunciation (*Caterina* etc), whereas the English sometimes has the stress on the **o**. The Gaelic spelling is a bit problematic, since it breaks the Gaelic rule of *broad to broad and slender to slender.*[11] But it has become the common spelling and can be regarded as an exception to the rule.

Ceilidh: an organised evening's entertainment of Highland music, storytelling etc usually held in a hotel, village hall or similar, and often conducted to some extent in English. Gaelic **cèilidh** 'a visit'. The traditional ceilidh, on the other hand, was an informal gathering of neighbours to chat and exchange gossip, often featuring stories and song, all usually in Gaelic. Most villages had a house marked for this purpose, the **taigh-cèilidh**, and such gatherings were an enjoyable way of passing the long winter nights. The Scots

---

Aberdeenshire, but not in the various examples of Balemeanach, also 'middle farm', both from **meadhan** 'middle'. Pitmedden reflects an earlier unlenited Gaelic form.

[11] When a consonant is flanked by vowels they must be slender only (e, i) or else broad only (a, o, u).

word *kailier* is used to describe a person who outstays his welcome and relates more to the traditional concept of a visit.

Ceòl mòr: pibroch, the classical music of the bagpipe. Gaelic **ceòl-mòr** 'great music'. See also under **pibroch**. **Ceòl** is related to *pipe*, being the Q-Celtic version (see under **cailleach**) with the second **p** disappearing as normally happens (**p** not being an original Gaelic letter).

There was a saying:

Cha robh ruidhle riamh am Boraraig
There was never a reel in Boreraig.

Boreraig, near Dunvegan, Skye, was the home of the piping college run by the MacCrimmons, hereditary pipers to MacLeod of Dunvegan. They taught only pibroch, **ceòl-mòr**, not light music, **ceòl-beag**, such as reels etc. See also under **reel** below.

Clabber: mud, mire, filth. Gaelic **clàbar**. This word is more common in Irish English but appears in Scots in various spellings, including *glabber*. The Irish poet Yeats, in *Countess Kathleen* says 'The dead leaves and clauber of four forests / Cling to my foot-sole'.

Clachan: a village; often appearing in Scots English as Kirkton. Gaelic **clachan**. The root of the word is **clach** 'stone', related to Latin *calcis*, *calculus*, 'pebble', English *calculate*.[12] Stone carving was widely practised to a high standard (crosses, ecclesiastical buildings, gravestones etc) in the Highlands and Islands from the 8th century to the late mediaeval period, and the surname Clacher survives, though the English translation Mason (Scots Masson) is far more common. Clachan appears quite often as a place-name – e.g. on Lismore – but usually has a more specific reference, e.g. Clachan of Glendaruel in Cowal.

---

[12] Originally *count using pebbles*, a system still used today by many cricket umpires to count the number of balls in an over.

Clan: a tribe having the same surname and a single chief. Gaelic **clann** 'children'. The word is related to Latin *planta* 'plant', 'offshoot', 'sprout' and shows the Q-Celtic version, as mentioned above under **cailleach**; so the Welsh for children is *plant*. Clans, not all of them of Gaelic origin, developed in Scotland from around 1100 A.D., and the word first appears in English in the 14th century. Most clans contain many members who have no relationship to the chief or ruling family but have become clan members for reasons of geography, protection, legality and general convenience.

Clann is not the modern Gaelic word for *clan*, however, **cinneadh** or **fine** being used instead. The latter will perhaps be familiar in the name of one of Ireland's main political parties, *Fine Gael*, 'Tribe of the Gaels'.

Clarsach: a Celtic harp. Gaelic **clàrsach**. This is an old instrument, commoner than the bagpipe in earlier centuries, but its use declined after the break-up of Gaelic society after 1745.[13] It was revived in the 20th century, however, and now enjoys considerable popularity. There is a saying:

Chan eil teud am chlàrsaich

There isn't a string in my harp meaning 'I'm useless, ineffectual'. Compare the English phrase (of opposite meaning) *another string to one's bow*. A player of the instrument is a **clàrsair**, but this has not survived as a surname in the way *Harper* has. But an earlier Celtic harp, the six-stringed **cruit**, now, in the form *crwth*, mostly associated with Wales, gives the surname MacWhirter **MacCruiteir**, while the Old English form *crowd* gives the surnames Crowther, Crowdson. There is a **Coire a' Chruiteir** 'Harper's Corrie' (see below under **corrie**) on Beinn Dòbhrain, mentioned by Duncan MacIntyre in his famous poem (line 79) about the mountain. Many readers will also be familiar with the words 'Harp of joy, o cruit mo chridhe' in the Eriskay love lilt.

---

[13] Even earlier in the south. Sir Walter Scott, in his poem *The Lay of the Last Minstrel* represents the 'infirm and old' minstrel singing his lay about 1700.

Claver: to gossip, idle chatter. Gaelic **clabair** 'a garrulous chatterer, babbler'. The root is **clab** 'an open mouth' from English *clap*, *clapper*, the latter also known as a tongue (of a bell), the source of the noise. Fr Allan McDonald in his collection of words mentioned below under **dulse** has **clàbhaist** 'a noisy conversation, everyone talking at once', (though the accent over the **a** suggests that this is an unrelated word).

Claymore: a large highland sword, usually double-edged and two-handed, but also applied to a single-handed sword. Gaelic **claidheamh-mòr** 'big sword'. The word is probably cognate with Latin *gladius* 'sword', English *gladiator* etc. They frequently appear on carved grave slabs and were obviously prized possessions. A proverb says:

Dà nì ro dhuilich an taghadh, bean agus claidheamh.
Two things very hard to choose, a wife and a claymore.

The famous sword of Sir Bevis of Hampton, *Morglay* is some-times cited, presumably thought to be formed from *claymore* but in the English way, with the adjective first, i.e. *moreclay*. But Sir Bevis features in an early mediaeval verse romance celebrating earlier Anglo-Saxon times, so perhaps Welsh *cleddyf* would be a likelier allusion; and though the clay-more appeared in Scotland in the late 15th century, the tradi-tional reference of *morglay* to French *glaive de la mort* 'sword of death' is more likely.

Dannsa a' Chlaidheimh is a well-known solo sword dance of some antiquity.

Mòr, familiar to most Scots from the many instances of Benmore / **Beinn Mhòr**, must be one of the commonest adjectives in the country's placenames.

cock (eyed): squinting. Gaelic **caog** 'to squint' has been suggested, but the borrowing is not clear. Adjectives are **caogach** and **caog-shùileach**, the latter featuring **sùil** 'eye', and the former appearing in the well-known pibroch **Lasan Phàdraig Chaogaich** 'A Flame of

Anger for Squinting Patrick' composed by Donald Mòr MacCrimmon.

Corkir: a lichen used in dyeing, giving a purple or red colour. Also korkir. Gaelic **corcar**, from Latin *purpura*. This is another instance of a Q-Celtic form, as mentioned under **cailleach**; Welsh, by contrast, has *porffor*. See also **crotal**, below.

Coronach: a dirge, lament, often at funerals. Gaelic **corranach**. The basis of this word is generally accepted to be **rànaich** 'crying, wailing' with the prefix **co-** (also found as **comh-**, **con-**) meaning *together*, implying group activity, as English *co-education*, *compartment* etc.

Corrie: a deep round hollow in a hill. Gaelic **coire** 'a cauldron', 'whirlpool'. The word appears in several placenames, as Corrour **Coire Odhar** 'Brown Corrie' north of Rannoch, and, as a whirlpool, Corryvreckan **Coire Bhreacain** 'Breacan's Cauldron' between Jura and Scarba.[14] **Coire** is one of the explanations of the surnames Corrie and Currie, presumably relating to an ancestor who lived or worked near a corrie. **Coire** is the normal everyday word for a kettle, though the English word (in its Norse form) appears in the name Torquil **Torcall,** Thor's kettle (Þórkætill, or, with the **t** lenited out, Þórkell) and the surnames MacCorquodale, MacCorkindale. Compare also **quaich**, below.

Cot: a small boat, usually for ferrying passengers across a river. Gaelic **coit**. Boat of Garten, near Aviemore, is **Coit a' Ghartain,** and the Cot House was an old inn on the River Echaig at the head of the Holy Loch, Cowal, where travellers were ferried across before a bridge was built.

Craig: a form of crag, cliff, steep rock face. This gives the Scottish names Craig, Craigie, Craik and Cragg, but the word is really a general Celtic one;

---

[14] Breacan was an early Irish warrior who is supposed to have sunk there with his fleet of fifty ships.

there are places in the north of England, as Blindcrake and Crayke, which have this word from Old British. The English poet Tennyson even uses it to describe the 'barren crags' of Ithaca at the beginning of his poem *Ulysses*. The fuller form in Gaelic is **carraig** 'rock', but the shorter form **creag** is probably more common. Both are found in dozens of place-names, as Carrick in Ayrshire, Cowal and Fife – it is also a surname – and Craignure **Creag an Iubhair,** 'Rock of the Yew Tree' in Mull.

Cran: a measure of fresh herring, a barrel of 37.5 gallons; also given as 28 stone, or 4 baskets, or an average of 1,200 fish. Gaelic **crann** 'a tree', 'plough'. The general idea is *wood*. Compare **crannog**, below, a round wooden structure, which can also mean 'a hamper, basket'. Since **crann** also means 'lot, lottery' – **An Crannchur Nàiseanta** is the National Lottery – it has been suggested that the custom of drawing lots to divide the catch may account for its use as a measure of herring.

Crannog: an island, often partly or wholly artificial, built on Scottish and Irish lochs to provide a measure of security to Bronze-age peoples, and connected to the mainland by a easily defended causeway. Gaelic **crannag**. Several continued in use into the middle ages. There are many in Loch Awe, in Argyll, and in Loch Tay, and elsewhere, though they are mostly now under water due to rising water levels (often due to hydro-electric dams), but Loch Tay has a modern recreation of a 'lived-in' crannog open to visitors. They were mostly built of wood, which is the basic meaning of **crann**.

Cranreuch: hoar frost. This word is thought to contain the Gaelic words **reothadh** 'frost' and **crann** 'shrivel', yet another meaning of **crann**, this time as a verb. An alternative Scots form *cranra*, the oldest form of the word, is slightly nearer the Gaelic. In his poem *To a Mouse* Burns wrote

Now thou's turned out...
To thole the winter's sleety
dribble, an' cranreuch cauld!

Creagh: a raid, plunder, booty. Also creach. Gaelic **creach**. There is a Ben Creach in the south of Mull which may have something to do with booty or raiding. A fairly common exclamation (now rather old-fashioned) is **mo chreach 's a thàinig** 'good grief!, dear me!'.

Creel: a wicker basket for fish, peat, seaweed etc. Dwelly gives an obsolete Gaelic word **criol** which looks like a borrowing from English; the normal Gaelic is **cliabh**. The wicker construction from rods, **slatan**, would allow any excess water to drain out. A proverb says:

Is cho math dol don tobar le cliabh

It's as well going to the well with a creel

i.e. it's pointless.

Crine: to shrink, shrivel. Gaelic **crìon** 'withered, shrunk'. This is probably the root of the placename Crinan (canal) in Argyll, **An Crìonan**, 'the withered area' and possibly also Crianlarich, south of Tyndrum, of similar meaning.

Cromack: a crook, a walking stick with a curved head. Also crummack, crummock. Gaelic **cromag**. The idea is *curved, bent*. See under **caschrom** and **crombie**. The word became familiar to many non-Gaels from its mention in the song *The Road to the Isles*:

The far Cuillins are pullin me away
As take I wi' my cromack to the road.

Crombie: a woollen overcoat or other garment. See under **caschrom** and **cromack.** There are several places called Crombie, a couple of them in Aberdeenshire; the cloth was manufactured in Aberdeen.

Crotal: a lichen used in dying wool etc. Also crottle. Gaelic **crotal**. Colours ranged from orange to dark brown and people had their own recipes for making the dyes. See also corkir, above.

29

Cuddy: 1. a young saithe or coalfish. Also cudden, cuddin. Gaelic **cudaig**, **cudainn**. The fish is also known as *cuithe* in Scots.

Cuddy: 2. an evening's entertainment due to a superior from his tenant, or payment in lieu. An obsolete historical term from Gaelic **cuid-oidhche** 'an evening's share'.

Culdee: an ascetic member of the Celtic church from the 8th to about the 13th century. The word means *servant* or *associate of god*. Modern Gaelic **cèile** and **dhè**, though the main meaning of the former now is *spouse*. They had a strong presence in Iona and other towns, and still apparently exist with the modern title *The Celtic Church of the Culdees*. Another survival is the placename Culdeesland near Methven, Perthshire. **Dhè** occurs in Dee in Aberdeenshire, the river Dee being **Uisge Dhè**, and there is another River Dee at Kirkcubright, Galloway, though in both the meaning is *goddess*, rivers usually having

been regarded as female deities.

Currach: a boat similar to a coracle. Also curragh. Gaelic **curach**. These were round or oval shaped in Wales, and were made of animal hides stretched over a wicker framework. There were also more elongated versions; Irish ones were more like canoes. Coracle itself is from Welsh *corwg*. Cambuscurrie Bay in the Dornoch Firth is though to be **Camas Curaidh** 'Coracle Bay'.

D

Dalradian: a geological term applied to pre-Cambrian rocks in the Highlands. From *Dalriada* Gaelic **Dàl Riata**, roughly Argyll at its fullest extent. This was the name given to this territory by Gaels from Dàl Riata in the northeast of Ireland in memory of their homeland. (See also under **Atholl**, above.)

Dalt: a foster child. Also dault. Gaelic **dalta**. Kildalton parish in Islay, home of the famous Kildalton cross, is the Church of the foster child, i.e. the disciple. Later fosterage became a well-established practice in Gaelic society to cement relationships between families

Deasil: in a sunwise direction, i.e. from east to west, left to right while facing south. Also deasiul, deasoil, deis(h)eal. Gaelic **deiseil**. The root of the word is **deas** 'south'. In earlier times in the Highlands and Islands tasks were carried out and people and buildings approached in this way, as it was felt to be lucky and would bring success to any undertaking. Nowadays the word is used to mean *ready, in good order, prepared* – an extension of its earlier meaning. **Deas** also means *right* (as opposed to *left*) and is cognate with English *dexter, dextrous*. The surname Deas is fairly common and originally indicated someone from the south; Dyce, a parish in Aberdeenshire and a surname, is a variant of it. It is also very common in place-names; South Uist, for instance, is **Uibhist a Deas**.

Deoch-an-doruis: a drink at the door on the way out, a stirrup cup, one for the road. Also doch-an-doris, doch-an-dorach, deuch-an-doris, and facetiously, Jock and Doris. Gaelic **deoch an dorais**, cited by Sir Harry Lauder in his well-known song beginning 'Just a wee deoch and dorais...'. Deochray, **deoch rèidh** 'smooth drink' is found in Scots to describe a form of sowens. (See below under **sowens**). **Doras**, which is cognate with English *door*, appears in Dorusduain, **Doras Dubhain** 'door i.e. opening, mouth, of the black burn', a couple of miles east of Loch Duich, and there is the notorious **Doras Mòr** between Loch Craignish out towards the open sea past Garbh Reisa on the south. A proverb begins:

> **Deoch an dorais,**
> **deoch an t-sonais,**
> **Deoch an deagh thurais**
> **dhuinn.**
> A drink at the door,
> a drink of happiness,

The drink for a good journey for us.

Dewar-flask: a vacuum flask, named after its inventor Sir James Dewar. Dewar is Gaelic **Deòir** from **deòradh** 'an exile', 'a pilgrim'. The word was used of those who went on pilgrimages, and then extended to those who had charge of holy relics. The forms Macindeoir **Mac an Deòir** and MacGeorge also occur. The word is found in the placenames Dewar near Dalkeith, Glenjorrie, near Glenluce in Dumfries and Galloway and Ballindeor (Balindore) on Loch Etive, Argyll.

Dod: ill temper, the sulks. Gaelic **dod** 'ill humour'.

Donald: world ruler. A male forename and surname. Gaelic **Dòmhnall**. **Domhan** is 'the universe', 'the deep', related to **domhain** 'deep', found in Baldovan **Ball Domhainn**, 'deep place' just north of Dundee, and various glens and corries in the Highlands; also Dunwich in England (Domnoc in 731, *-wich* being added later), 'deep water' from Old British. The Scots form Donal is nearer the Gaelic since it doesn't have the final **d** often added to Gaelic names taken into English as Dugald (Gaelic **Dùghall**), Lamond (Gaelic **Laomainn**) etc. So Ferindonald in Skye is **Fearann Dòmhnaill** 'Donald's Land', and similarly with Cardonald, Dundonald etc.

Donsie: a word of various meanings, including unlucky, glum, feeble (minded), bad-mannered, neat, self-important. The word is based on Gaelic **donas** 'bad luck', 'mischief', the opposite of **sonas** 'good fortune, happiness'. See under **sonsie** below. **Dona** 'bad' occurs in Lochdonhead, **Ceann Loch Dona** in Mull. The **s / d** interchange of opposites is quite common in Gaelic, as **saor** 'cheap', **daor** 'dear'; **soirbh** 'easy', **doirbh** 'difficult' etc.

Dorlach: a bundle, a handful. Gaelic **dòrlach**. The root of the word is **dòrn** 'fist' and the diminutive **dòirneag** is 'pebble, a stone to fit in your fist'. This is the origin of the several placenames Dornoch and Dornie, although Dwelly has **dòrnaidh** to mean a narrow channel of the sea.

Dorlach contains the suffix -*lach* with the meaning *a collection of, lots of*, and so means 'a fistful'; similarly **teaghlach**, from **taigh** and -*lach* is 'a houseful, household, family'. The suffix -*lach* is from **sluagh** in the sense 'a host of, lots of' (see below under **slew**); the dropping (and sometimes adding) of an initial **s** is a feature of Gaelic (and of English!).

Dougal(l), **Dugald**: dark foreigner. A male forename and surname. Gaelic **Dùghall**, from **dubh** 'black', 'dark' and **gall** 'a stranger', a Dane, distinguished from the fair-haired Norse and Swedes. The name also appears as MacDougal(l), MacDowel and Doyle, the last being mainly Irish. South Morar is known in Gaelic as **Mòrar Mhic Dhùghaill**. The main use of **Gall** today is to mean a Lowland Scot, a non-Gael, and **A'**

Ghalltachd is the Lowlands of Scotland. **Gall** is found in several placenames, the most well known being **a' Ghall-Ghàidhealtachd** Galloway, **Innse Gall** Hebrides and **Gallaibh** Caithness.

Dubh gives the surnames Dow and Dove, (Mac)Duff, Duffy and Duffus, and is very common in placenames but possibly the best known, The Black Isle, is deceptive in that it's not an island and it's not directly from **dubh** 'black', but named after St Dubhthach, the remains of whose church can still be seen there.

Douglas: Dark or black burn. A male forename and surname. Gaelic **Dùbhghlas** from **dubh** 'black' and **glais** 'stream', the latter now obsolete,[15] though it features in placenames such as the parish of Glass in Aberdeenshire and Kinglassie in Fife. Douglas is a town in Lanarkshire, as well as the capital of the Isle of Man, and is descriptive, but sometimes a place refers to the surname, as Castle Douglas, south

---

[15] But still found in Manx as *glass*.

west of Dumfries, and Douglastown, just south of Forfar. Douglas Water in Lanarkshire is a good example of a tautology where water 'explains' the forgotten *glas*. The same thing happens in England with Dowles Brook and Dawlish Water, both from the Old British form of Gaelic **Dùbhghlas**.

As a surname, Douglas appears also as Dewlish in England. A Douglas fir is an American tree introduced to Scotland by David Douglas in the 19th century.

Drab: a slut. Gaelic **dràbag** and **dràbair**, female and male respectively. There is some uncertainty, however, whether the English word is from Gaelic or vice versa. The word is not particularly heard much in either language, but the related **drabasta** 'obscene' is common in Gaelic.

Drambuie®: a whisky liqueur. This is the registered trademark of a particular product, and its inclusion is presumably due to its more established position, and other liqueurs might feel aggrieved to have been excluded.[16] See also **Glenlivet** below. The word is from *dram* 'a small alcohol-based drink' and **buidhe** 'yellow'. *Dram* is a shortened form of drachma, a Greek currency (until the advent of the Euro) and a unit of weight. **Buidhe** is common in place names, as Lochbuie in the south of Mull, or Achiltibuie, north west of Ullapool. Buie is also a surname, though rare; more common is Bowie. The form preceded by **mac gille** 'son of the servant' (common in Gaelic surnames) gives **MacGilleBhuidhe**, MacElvee, Gilbey. The name presumably originally meant flaxen haired.

Drammock: a mixture of oatmeal and cold water, also drammach. Gaelic **dramaig, dramach** 'crowdie'. Another case where there is some uncertainty whether the English word is from Gaelic or vice versa, but it has been used in Scots since the 16th century.

---

[16] In the same way Coca-Cola is in the dictionary, but not any other cola drink.

Droich: a dwarf. Gaelic **troich, droich**, the former being the normal form today. The form *drochle* is common in Scots. Scots also has *dwerch* which is related to English *dwarf*, and it may be that **droich** is due to metathesis (letters changing their place in a word), which is a feature of Scots, as *girse / grass, girdle / griddle* etc.

Drum: a ridge. Gaelic **druim** 'back' (of a person or beast), 'ridge'. The word is related to Latin *dorsum* 'back', English *dorsal*, with the Gaelic form featuring metathesis again (see the previous entry). Drum is very common in placenames, as Tyndrum **Taigh an Droma**, 'The House on the Ridge' in Argyll, and Drymen in Stirlingshire. The surname Drummond, **Druiminn**, itself from a placename, is also common. Geologists will be familiar with the related word *drumlin*, an elongated ridge formed during the last ice age. Less well-known nowadays is Drummond light, another name for limelight, invented by T. Drummond in the 19th century.

Duan: a section of a poem. Gaelic **duan** 'a poem'. A famous example is the **Duan Albanach** 'Scottish poem', of around 1100, giving a largely fabulous list of the Kings of Scotland.

Dulse: an edible seaweed. Gaelic **duileasg**. The root of the word seems to be **duille**, more commonly **duilleag**, 'a leaf'. Other edible seaweeds are carragheen, also known as Irish moss, Gaelic **carraigean**; tangle, Gaelic **stamh**; and sloke, Gaelic **slòcan, slabhcan**. Seaweed was also used in the kelp industry from the late 1700s up to about 1830 to make iodine and potash. The Hebrides are, of course, a rich source of seaware; Fr Allan McDonald lists over 30 terms for seaweed in his collection of words from South Uist and Eriskay, and a saying about Ulva, off Mull is

Bàrr òir a' cuartachadh Eilean Ulbhaigh

A crop of gold surrounding the island of Ulva.

– a reference to seaweed.

Dun: greyish-brown. Gaelic **donn** 'brown'. The English and Gaelic words are related but it is unclear whether one has influenced the other, or whether they evolved separately. This is one of the origins of the surname Dunn, referring to brown hair, and this is still a common usage today. It also appears in placenames, as Knockdon, **An Cnoc Donn** 'The Brown Hill', just north of Bridgend in Islay and Tomdoun, **An Tom Donn** 'The Brown Hillock' on Loch Garry in Inverness-shire.

Duncan: Brown warrior. A male forename and a surname. Gaelic **Donnchadh** from **donn** 'brown' and **cath** 'battle'. Hence the surnames Donachie and MacConnachie (various spellings), the latter without the initial **d** sound since the **d** has been lenited, the same feature as found in the surname MacConnel, Gaelic **MacDhòmhnaill** (MacDonald). This clan is also known as Robertson, after a Robert who lived in the 14th century, but in Gaelic the Robertsons are **Clann Donnchaidh**, keeping the name of the original founder in the 13th century. The name appears in Toberonochy[17] **Tobar Dhonnchaidh** 'Duncan's Well' on Luing, and Duncansburgh was one of the earlier names of Fort William.

Dun(n)iwassal: a minor Highland nobleman, a gentleman of high birth. Also duniewassal. Gaelic **duine** 'man', **uasal** 'high'. The latter, in its Welsh form *uchel* appears in several places, the most well-known being the Ochil Hills, and Ochiltree, near Ayr, and the surname Ogilvie or Ogilvy was originally a placename in Angus, meaning 'high plain'; modern Welsh has *uchelfa* 'a high place'.[18] For placenames modern Gaelic prefers the related forms **uarach** (**Col Uarach**, Upper Coll, and **Pabail Uarach**, Upper Bayble, both in Lewis) and uachdrach (Kinuachdrach, **An**

---

[17] **D** is often silent after **r** in placenames; so Inveruglas **Inbhir Dhubhghlais**, at the north end of Loch Lomond, Inveroran **Inbhir Dhobhrain**, near Bridge of Orchy, etc.

[18] A single **f** in Welsh is voiced, i.e. sounded like an English **v**.

Ceann Uachdrach, at the north end of Jura.

E

Eirack: a pullet, a young hen. Gaelic **eireag**. **An Eireag Mhanannach** 'The Calf of Man' is the name of a small island just to the south of the Isle of Man, and just to the south of it is the Chicken Rock. It features in the saying **A' Chearc Leòdhasach, an Coileach Arannach agus an Eireag Mhanannach** 'The Hen of Lewis, the Cock of Arran and the Pullet of Man', all of which might be seen in a day's sailing but only in ideal conditions. The Hen of Lewis is Chicken head on the Eye Peninsula (Point), and the Cock of Arran is at the north tip of the island. Gaelic has many sayings involving three things – see, for instance, under **bard** above. People of certain islands and districts were also traditionally called after birds and animals. **Eireag** was a name for people from Kerrera, Benderloch in Argyll, and Isle Oronsay on Skye. A Gaelic equivalent of *the cart before the horse* is the Mull saying **ubh air tòir eireig** 'an egg chasing a pullet'.

Ewen: well-born. A male forename and a surname. Also Ewan, Euan. Gaelic **Eòghann**. The name Eugene, in its various European forms has the same meaning. The first part may be related to Greek eu 'well, good' (*eu*logy, *eu*phemism etc) and the second part is cognate with English *gene*, *gene*alogy etc. The form Eunson is quite common in Scotland while Ewing has more of an Irish flavour. Immeroin, **Iomaire Eòghainn,** 'Ewen's Ridge of Land' just south of Loch Voil in Perthshire reflects the Gaelic form of the name much more than Balmakewan (Marykirk) in the Mearns and Tullichewen at the foot of Loch Lomond.

F

Fail: a turf, sod. Gaelic **fàl.** A fail dyke is a turf wall, and **fàl** can mean a wall or dyke in Gaelic. There is some disagreement about whether this word originated in Gaelic or in Scots. The word is cognate with Latin *vallum* 'rampart', from which comes English *wall*. As the form *wall* indicates, it was borrowed into Anglo-Saxon at a time when Latin **v** was pronounced **w** (its usual pronunciation up to about the 2nd or 3rd century A.D.); the Gaelic, however, (and the other Celtic forms) goes back to an Indo-European root. The **w** sound was preserved in Old British words borrowed from British Latin as a more correct formal pronunciation, though the **v** sound existed colloquially. Anglo-Saxon took the word from Old British.

The presence of Old Irish *fál* suggests that Scots was the borrower; Old Irish would not have borrowed from Scots, and an original Scots form would have been nearer to the English *wall*. The Antonine wall, also known as Grahame's (or Grimes) dyke, built across Scotland in the 2rd century A.D was a turf wall, and **fàl** features in several placenames, the most interesting of which is Kinneil,

Ceann an Fhàil[19], 'End of the Wall' near Bo'ness at the eastern end of the Antonine Wall. Kinneil has its equivalent / translation, Wallsend, at the eastern end of Hadrian's wall. Although Wallsend is only about 100 miles from Kinneil, the English form well illustrates the eventual predominance, particularly in the east of England, of that language over native Old British. Wallsend, first attested in the 11th century, would have been called Penguaul or similar before English speakers renamed it. Old British did, of course, survive in many placenames elsewhere in England. Rhifail **An Ruigh Fàil** 'The Slope with a Dyke' is in Strath Naver, Sutherland, and Dunphail **Dùn Fàil** 'Fort with a Rampart' is south of Forres in Moray.

Fank: a sheep fold, pen. Gaelic **fang**. Another word of debated origin, the possibility that it may be from Scots *fank* being strengthened by its absence from Gaelic

---

[19] Another instance of a lenited **f** with the **f** sound disappearing.

placenames. Other words for a sheepfold are **crò** and **buaile;** the former appears for instance in Craw in the north-west of Arran and Badachro near Gairloch in Ross and Cromarty, while the latter is found in Boltachan, **Bualtachan,** near Aberfeldy, Perthshire. On the other hand fank isn't attested in written Scots before the 19th century, *fauld* (English *fold*) being the common Scots long before that.[20] And the fact that *fank* appears in Manx, as do **crò** and **buaile** (*cro* and *bwoaillagh*) suggests that it is unlikely to have come from Scots.

Farquhar: very dear, friendly, or, man friendly depending on whether the first element is **fear** 'man' or, more likely, an old Gaelic preverb with the sense of *over, very much.* The second element is **càr** 'friendly', more commonly appearing as **caraid** 'friend', cognate with English *caress, charity,* Italian *caro,* French *cher* etc. A male forename and

surname. The Gaelic form is **Fearchar**. The old Scots spelling *quh* for English *wh* is now found only in surnames or place names, as Farquhar, Colquhoun, Sanquhar etc but has changed its pronunciation. Farquhar is nowadays pronounced something like *Farker* or *Farcher*, and other forms of the name, as MacKerchar, MacErchar, (**MacFhearchair**) are nearer to the Gaelic sound.[21] Farquharson is a small settlement in Kincardineshire.

Feis: a Celtic arts festival. Gaelic **fèis**. Such festivals go back a long way in Irish history, but have recently become popular in the Highlands and Islands, a bit like Highland games, in as much as there usually seems to be one taking place somewhere. The word is from Latin *festia* and is related to English *festival, feast* and *fête.* The form **fèist** (formerly **fèisd**) is also found but is used

---

[20] There are quite a number of Faulds placenames in the south of the country.

[21] The **f** has disappeared from MacKerchar and MacErchar in accordance with the absence of sound of a lenited **f** in Gaelic.

in the more general sense of a *feast* or *banquet*. The general word for a festival is **fèill**.

Fenella: an English form of **Fionnaghal** 'white shoulder', from **fionn** 'white, fair' and **gualainn** or **guala** 'shoulder'. A female forename. Another, and more common, anglicisation is Flora, although this is the name of the Roman goddess of flowers and has nothing to do with **Fionnaghal**. This happens quite a lot with Gaelic names where the traditional English version is not a translation, but means something quite different; some examples are **Gilleasbuig** 'Archibald', **Tormod** 'Norman', **Eachainn** 'Hector', **Ruairidh** 'Derek', **Ùisdean** 'Hugh', **Ùna** 'Winifred', **Mòr(ag)** 'Sarah', **Raonaid** 'Rachel', **Beathag** 'Sophie'.

Fenella became more widely known after Sir Walter Scott used it as the name of a character in his novel *Peveril of the Peak*, although any Scottish connections are obscure since she was the daughter of the Englishman Edward Christian and a Moorish woman.

Fionn is very common in placenames, and **gualainn** occurs as a topographical feature meaning 'shoulder of a hill', 'long ridge' and appears in Guailainn, just east of Kinlochbervie in Sutherland, and Gualachulain, **Guala Chuilinn** 'Ridge of Holly' at the head of Loch Etive in Argyll. Strath Finella (another spelling) in the Mearns was named after Fenella, wife of a local **mormaor** (see below under **mormaor**), who was involved in the murder of Kenneth II in 995.

Fergus: superior choice, or, man choice. A male forename and basis of a surname. See under **Farquhar** for the first part of the word and **Angus** for the second. Gaelic **Fearghas**. Other forms are Fergus(s)on and MacKerras (**MacFhearghais**), the latter showing the disappearance of a lenited **f** (see also under Farquhar). The name occurs in a few placenames, as St Fergus, just north of Peterhead, and

Tullyfergus near Alyth, Perthshire.

Filibeg: a kilt. Also filabeg, fillibeg. Gaelic **fèileadh-beag** 'small kilt', although **fèileadh** usually appears without **beag** in modern Gaelic. English spellings with initial **ph** also occur but are wrong, as can be seen from the Gaelic. The combination **ph** does occur in Gaelic (a lenited **p**) and represents an original **p**[22] but English transliterations of Gaelic **ph** as **f** are misleading also. For example, *McFall* for Gaelic **MacPhàil** rather obscures the origin of the word, which is the name *Paul*. **Fèileadh** is cognate with English *veil*, meaning *a covering*, itself ultimately from Latin *velum*. The Kilt Rock in Staffin, Skye is a cliff face resembling the folds of a kilt, best viewed from the sea.

Finlay: fair hero. A male forename and surname. Gaelic **Fionnlagh** from **fionn** 'white,

fair' and **laoch** 'hero'. The form MacKinlay (**MacFhionnlaigh**) shows the normal disappearance of a lenited **f**. An alternative spelling Findlay has the typical intrusive **d** found in Scottish versions of English names, e.g. Hen**d**ry.

Finn: fair(haired). A male forename and basis of a surname (Finnie). Gaelic **Fionn**. Fionn Mac Cumhail was the legendary hero of Celtic epics, loosely attributed to the 3rd century A.D., and the father of Ossian. In the 18th century James MacPherson anglicised his name as Fingal, using it as the title of one of his Ossianic epics, which he claimed controversially were based on old Gaelic ballads and other tales. His work achieved great popularity, being translated into other European languages, but doubts have remained how much of his poems were of genuine antiquity – which was certainly the case – and how much was a figment of his own imagination. Fingal's cave on Staffa is well-known to tourists, including Mendelssohn, who used its name for an overture,

---

[22] For this reason Latin or Greek words borrowed by Gaelic have **f** for **ph** of the classical languages; so philosophia 'philosophy' is **feallsanachd**.

also known as *The Hebrides*, written in 1830 after a visit there.

Fiona could also be mentioned here. This word used as a female forename was another invention of James MacPherson, and achieved prominence from its use as a penname (Fiona MacLeod) by William Sharp (1855-1905), a poet and biographer who edited MacPherson's works. It presumably means 'fair' and does not readily conform to Gaelic spelling or pronunciation rules.

Finnock: a young sea trout, a grilse. Also finnack, finnac. Gaelic **fionnag**. The more common word is **bànag**, but both words are based on the meaning *white*, and both have the diminutive indicator **-ag** of feminine nouns.

Fiorin: a type of grass, variously described as sea bent, a type of bent grass, and couch grass. Gaelic **fioran**, **freothainn**.

G

Gadhel: a Gael, a Celtic speaker from Scotland, Ireland and the Isle of Man. Also Goidel. Gaelic **Gàidheal**. The adjective *Gadhelic* (also *Goidelic*) describes Q-Celtic (see under **cailleach** above).

Gael: a Gaelic-speaking Scottish Highlander, although the word can also be used to refer to a Gadhelic-speaker. Gaelic **Gàidheal**. The adjective Gaelic, **Gàidhealach**, is also found with *coffee* (also known as Irish coffee, coffee with whisk(e)y added) and football (a 15-a-side round ball game played in Ireland). The word features in placenames such as Argyll (see above), Fleenasnagael, just south of Nairn, and, possibly, Cargill, a few miles north of Perth.

Gàidhealtachd: a Gaelic-speaking area, traditionally the Highlands and (Western) islands of the country, so this would not include, for instance, Glasgow, which has large numbers of Gaelic speakers, though not as many as it used to, although the current expansion of Gaelic-medium education may restore numbers there. The word appears in Chambers in its Gaelic spelling, to distinguish it from Gaeltacht (*Gaedhealtacht*), the Irish-speaking parts of Ireland. Its normal translation is *Highland*; the Highland Region of local government is **Roinn na Gàidhealtachd**. See also **kyloe** below.

Gallowglass: A mercenary soldier from the Western Isles who fought in Ireland from about the 14th to the 16th century. Also Galloglass. Gaelic **Gall-òglach** 'foreign soldier'. **Gall** is a stranger, foreigner, as such mercenaries would have seemed to the Irish. It is now the modern word for a lowland Scot, a non-Gael, and **A' Ghalltachd** is the Lowlands of Scotland. **Òglach** is from the root **òg** 'young' (which gives the surname Ogg, and, in Ireland, Hogan) with the suffix -*lach* mentioned under **dorlach** above. Surnames from **Gall** include Gall itself, and its variants Gault and Gaw, Galloway (also a

placename, see below), Galbraith (a stranger Briton, i.e. a non-Gaelic inhabitant of Strathclyde up to the early middle ages), MacGill[23], and the Irish Gallacher. There are several other placenames featuring **Gall**; best known are probably Camusnagaul, **Camas nan Gall** 'Bay of the Foreigners' across Loch Linnhe from Fort William, and **Innse Gall** 'The Hebrides'.

Galloway: a breed of black cattle; a type of small strong horse. Galloway is **A' Ghall-Ghàidhealtachd**, named after its inhabitants, the **Gall Gàidheal** 'Foreign Gael'. These were a mixture of Norse and Scots, who settled in Galloway in the late 9th and 10th centuries A.D. An inhabitant of Galloway is a Galwegian. Galloway appears in the English placename Galgate (Galwaithegate in the 12th century) 'The Galloway Gate' i.e. road, by the M6 motorway today, indicating the route for drovers etc to and

---

[23] One derivation of the name is **Mac a' Ghoill**, where **goill** is the genitive of **gall**.

from Galloway. The same idea is found today in the placename Scotch Corner on the other side of England.

Galore: enough, plenty. Gaelic **gu leòr**. The English use of the word usually follows the Gaelic idiom, coming immediately after its noun, as *Whisky Galore*, but it has also developed as a noun in English, meaning *an abundance of*.

Garron: a small sturdy horse. Also garran. Gaelic **gearran** 'a gelding, a castrated horse'. The root is the verb **geàrr** 'cut, shorten' which appears in a few placenames, notably Gare Loch, off the Firth of Clyde, and Gairloch on the west coast of Ross and Cromarty, both sea lochs, and both meaning *short loch*. Gair also occurs as a surname, common in the north-west, and sometimes found as Gear.

Garvie: a sprat. Gaelic **garbhag.** This is another word of uncertain origin. The diminutive indicator -*ie*, at the end of a word is a feature of Scots, but the alternative form *garvock* looks as if it is borrowed from Gaelic, with its **-ag** diminutive ending. **Garbhag** also means *a flounder*, and Fr. Allan McDonald[24] describes it as 'a flounder with a rough back', suggesting a connection with **garbh** 'rough', which would favour a Gaelic origin. Inchgarvie in the Firth of Forth is also probably 'rough island' despite earlier efforts to connect it with garvies.

Gillespie: Servant of the bishop. Gaelic **Gille Easbaig**. A male forename and a surname. A very large number of names begin with *Gill*, sometimes with *Mac + Gill*. See also **gillie**, below. **Easbaig** is a borrowing from Latin *episcopus*, as is English *episcopal* etc. It is found in the placenames Balnespick about five miles north-west of Kingussie, Bohespick near Blair Atholl, Perthshire, and in the surname Macanespie, **Mac an Easbaig** 'Son of the Bishop'.

---

[24] In his collection of South Uist and Eriskay words, see above under dulse.

Gillie: a guide or attendant in Highland pursuits such as fishing, deerstalking etc. Also gilly, ghillie, the latter being a misguided attempt to make the word seem more Gaelic by the erroneous insertion of the letter **h**. Gaelic **gille** 'boy, lad'. Historically the word was used to mean a servant, of indeterminate age, in a chief's retinue. As indicated in the previous entry, **gille** is often added to the name of a saint or other cleric; it is also sometimes added after **mac**, in which case the **g** is usually dropped. So MacLennan is **MacIllFhinnein** 'Son of the servant of St Finnan', MacLean is **MacIllEathain** 'Son of the servant of St John', and so on. **Gille** also occurs in placenames, as Gilmerton[25] 'The Farmstead of the Servant of the Virgin Mary' near Edinburgh and Gilston 'The Servant's Farm' in Midlothian. It is also found in England, as Gilsland in Cumbria, though **gille** may have become a personal name there.

---

[25] **Gille Moire** is also anglicised as Gilmour or Gilmore.

See also **Keelie** below.

Glassite: a member of a religious sect founded in the 18th century by John Glas(s). **Glas** means *grey* or *green*, or a combination of the two, and is the origin of the surname Glass, probably referring to a greying complexion, or perhaps an item of dress. Other forms of the name are Glasson and MacGlashan. There is also the possibility of old Gaelic **glas** 'a stream', mentioned under **Douglas**, above, as a source. Both words are common in placenames; **Glas Maol** 'Grey rounded Hill' is a Munro (see under **Munro**, below) in Angus. Glasgow, however, is Brythonic, from a form of Old British spoken in the area at the time, and means 'green hollow'; *glas* is also the Welsh word for green / grey.

Glen: a narrow hilly valley, usually with a river flowing down. Gaelic **gleann**. Glen can be contrasted with **strath** (see below under **strath**) which is a wider, often less hilly, valley. Glens are associated with Scotland (hence its use in various

'Scotch' whiskies from around the world, as *Glen Highland* from China) and Ireland and also, not surprisingly, reappear in parts of the former British Empire. Rather more surprising are the villages *Great Glen* and *Glen Parva* in England[26], but these are from an Old British form which appears in modern Welsh as *glyn*. *Glen* is occasionally used of towns and villages in this country, as Glenluce, a few miles east of Stranraer, and Glenrothes, in Fife, the latter being unusual in not having a real glen nearby, but, of course, it is a made-up name given to the new town. Glen(n) is a common surname, and also a male forename; another form is Glennie. Glendinning, a Dumfriesshire placename, is also a surname, sometimes spelled Glendenning.

Glengarry: a narrow woollen brimless bonnet, usually with a couple of short ribbons hanging at the back, worn by some Highland regiments. Glen Garry, **Gleann Garadh** 'Coppice Glen' lies just west of the Great Glen, and was the ancestral home of the MacDonells.

Glenlivet®: a Speyside whisky. This is the registered trademark of the products of this distillery in Banffshire. Gaelic **Gleann Liobhait**, meaning Glen of Water or Flooding. The Gaelic form indicates the local pronunciation, ($\mathbf{i} =$ English *ee*) as do the lines by the 19th century poet W.E. Aytoun in his capricious poem *The Massacre of the Macpherson*, written in mock-Highland English:

Fhairson had a son
  who married Noah's daughter,
And nearly spoiled ta Flood
  by drinking up ta water:
Which he would have done
  I at least pelieve it,
Had the mixture peen
  only half Glenlivet.

Glom: to snatch. Gaelic **glàm** 'to gobble up', 'seize'. The word is more common in

---

[26] The Great Glen, **An Gleann Mòr**, in Scotland is another name for the fault valley which stretches from Fort William to Inverness, about sixty miles, the route of the Caledonian Canal, also known as Glen More and Glen Albyn.

America, possibly influenced by Scots *glaum*, which is roughly the pronunciation of **glàm**.

Gob: the mouth. Generally thought to be from Gaelic **gob**, which nowadays means *a beak* or *bill*. A gobstopper is a large round sweet, and gobsmacked means *astonished*.

Goidel: See under **Gadhel**, above.

Gralloch: to disembowel deer, a deer's entrails. Gaelic **greallach**, 'entrails'.

H

Hamish: a follower, from Hebrew *Jacob*. A male forename. In its Latin form this word appeared as both *Jacobus* (hence *Jacobite* etc) and *Jacomus* (hence Italian *Giacomo*, etc). The English *James* is from the latter; Gaelic **Seumas** is a phonetic rendering of *James*. The vocative[27] case **Sheumais** has given rise to the Anglicised *Hamish*, though its general use in English is really incorrect, though by now well established; it is far more common in Scotland than the forms *Seumas* and the Americanised *Shamus*.

Hoolachan: a reel, the reel of Tulloch. Also hoolican. Gaelic **Thulachain**; the dropping of the **t** sound is a normal feature of a lenited **t** in Gaelic. The Reel of Tulloch, **Ruidhle Thulachain** is an old tune and a dance of several different forms. **Tulach** 'hillock' is very common in placenames in the Highlands, taking the forms Tulli-, Tully- and Tilly- in English. The English medical term **tylosis**, a lump, swelling, inflammation is from the same root. See also **tulchan**, below.

---

s, reflecting Indo-European usage, where the same word begins in some languages with **s** and in others with **h**. **Sock** 'a ploughshare', 'a snout' (hence the placename Succoth, by Strachur, a tapering piece of land between the junction of two streams) mentioned in the introduction, is an example. It derives from old Celtic **soc** 'pig'. The English cognate is *hog*.

Hubbub: a confused noise of many people talking at once, an uproar. For the former sense compare the similar sound of the English use of the word *rhubarb* to provide a nonsensical conversation to an audience in a theatre etc. The word is thought to reflect old Gaelic, or earlier Irish **ub ub** or similar, an interjection of derision.

I

Iain: John, a male forename and surname from Hebrew meaning *God is gracious*, or similar. Also Ian. MacIans were a branch of the MacDonalds and lived in Glencoe, where about 38 of them were killed in the massacre of 1692. Other forms of the name are **Eòin** and **(S)eathain**, the later found only in placenames, as Killean, **Cill Eathain** 'Church of St John', on Lismore.

Inch: an island, a stretch of grassland beside a river. Gaelic **innis**, cognate with English *insular*. The modern Gaelic word for island is **eilean**, but **innis** remains in many placenames, as **Innse Gall** 'Hebrides', *Inchmurrin* 'St Mirren's Isle', in Loch Lomond, *Inchmahome* 'St Colman's Isle' in the Lake of Menteith. As a meadow it appears in Inch in Edinburgh and the North Inch and South Inch in Perth. In its meaning of *island* the word also occurs in England as *Ince* in a couple of placenames, as well as *Inskip*, but this is from Old British; the modern Welsh for island is *ynys*, so *Ynys Wyth* is the Isle of Wight. For historical reasons the vast majority of Scotland's offshore islands feature neither **innis** nor **eilean**, but rather the Norse *ey*, Anglicised as *-ay* or *-a*; so *Soay, Barra etc*. The surnames Inch, Insch and Innes are from **innis**.

Ingle: a fire(place). Gaelic **aingeal** 'a fire'; also **ainneal**. Burns uses the word in *The Cotter's Saturday Night*:

His wee bit ingle, blinkin bonilie,
His clean hearth-stane…

where *ingle* is the fire. In Scots the fireplace is usually the *ingle-neuk* or *ingle-cheek*. The word is rather old-fashioned, and in Gaelic too the modern word for fire is **teine** or **gealbhan**, while the fireplace / hearth is **cagailt** or **teallach**. **Aingeal** is one of these words which featured in Highland superstitions. **Teine** was regarded as a taboo word which, since it described a dangerous thing, should be referred to only by a euphemistic synonym, in this case **aingeal**. The fact that the word also means *angel* would have helped. Such taboos were particularly common among fishermen, who were reluctant to call almost anything by its proper name, and this habit was not, of course, restricted to Scotland.[28]

Aingeal occurs in placenames but since it is also the word for *angel* (from a different root) the two meanings are sometimes confused. **Dùn** (or **Tom**) **Aingeal**, however, a few miles east of Spean Bridge, is generally regarded as *Beacon Hill*. This is the site of **Cill Choireil,** 'St Cyril's Church'

---

[28] It is still found in certain trades / professions; actors, for example do not like to refer to Shakespeare's *Macbeth* except by the phrase the *Scottish play*.

where Ian Lom the Keppoch bard is buried.

Inverness: an overcoat with a hood. The Gaelic for the town and county is **Inbhir Nis,** or, in Uist, **Eileir Nis**. *Inver*, a confluence of two streams, or of a river and the sea, is, of course, very common in placenames, and is the Gaelic equivalent of the Welsh and Old British *aber* which appears mainly in the east of the country (the old Pictland), as Aberdeen, Abernethy, etc. It is quite a common feature of Gaelic for the **v** sound to be dropped from **inbhir**, and this has resulted in placenames such as Innerpeffray, near Crieff, Innerleithen in the Borders, etc.

Ishbel: this name is a form of Elizabeth, but is now regarded as a separate name in its own right. Gaelic **Iseabail**. A female forename. The English spelling *Ishbel* represents the sound a Gaelic **s** makes when next to a slender vowel, which also accounts for the **sh** in the word *Hamish* mentioned above, and *Sheena* and *Shona* below.

K

Keel: ruddle, a red ochre used by weavers and sheep farmers. Gaelic **cìl**. The origin of this word is disputed, and it is marked as obsolete in Dwelly. The fact that it is found as an English dialect word suggests that Gaelic is the borrower.

Keelie: a word used to describe a rough character, an urban male of criminal tendencies, particularly one from Glasgow; another form of **gille** (see above).

Keen: a lament; to bewail the dead. Gaelic **caoin** 'to weep, wail'. Poetry for such occasions in Scotland and Ireland was called **caoineadh** or **cumha**. Keening has long died out, though recordings have been made of it, just as they have of waulking songs, another obsolete custom. It was much opposed by the church, especially in Ireland, though the church took a more tolerant view of other related activities, such as that mentioned in a Skye saying:

Cha robh fichead duine air mhisg air tiodhlac do sheanar.

There weren't even twenty drunk men at your grandfather's funeral.

A poor show, in other words. Keening, however, was a mainly female practice. In view of the treatment of initial Indo-European initial **k** mentioned above (under **caman**) it is not surprising that *whine*, the English cognate of **caoin**, does not have the **c** sound.

Kelpie: a water-horse. Thought to be from **cailpeach** or **colpach** 'a cow', 'a young horse'. As the **p** indicates this is not an original Gaelic word, but is from Norse. The Scots word colpindach, also meaning *cow*, is related to it, as is calp, a payment in kind paid by a tenant to his clan chief or superior. Modern Gaelic for a kelpie is simply **each-uisge** 'water horse'.

Kelvin: a temperature scale, named after Lord Kelvin, professor of Natural Philosophy in Glasgow University. The Kelvin district of

Glasgow is **Caol Abhainn**, the 'narrow river' which runs through it. For **caol** see under **Kyle**, below. **Abhainn** is the Gaelic form of the Celtic word found in Avon, the name of several rivers in England and Wales as well as one in Lanarkshire and one in Stirlingshire.

Kenneth: fair, handsome. Gaelic **Coinneach**. A male forename. The basis of this word is **cannach** 'pretty, fair' with the same root as that found in **canna**, mentioned above. The surname MacKenzie is from **Coinneach**, as the Gaelic form **MacCoinnich** makes clearer, revealing that the **z** in MacKenzie isn't an English **z**, but rather the old Scots letter yogh, pronounced like a **y** in this instance. Other rarer forms of the surname, *MacKenney* and *MacWhinney* look a bit nearer to the Gaelic for modern readers. Other surnames with yogh are *Dalziel* and *Menzies*. *Kenneth* is also sometimes thought to be derived from an early Gaelic **Cinaed** (or similar) meaning 'sprung from fire' (see under **Aedan**, above), but this has not survived as a modern

Gaelic forename, though surviving as surnames *MacKinney* and *MacKenna*.

Kilmarnock: a flat woollen bonnet, usually, blue, but also black or red, rather like a *balmoral* (see above under **balmoral**). The town is Gaelic **Cill Mheàrnaig** 'The Church of my Ernoc', i.e. Ernan (various spellings); the ending **-oc** is an affectionate diminutive, common in saints' names. There were over twenty saints with this name, which occurs again in several placenames, as Ardmarnock in Cowal and Inchmarnock, an island off the west-coast of Bute. **Cill**, anglicised as *Kil*, is from Latin *cella*, a monastic cell, and was used historically to mean *a church* or *churchyard* (more usual modern Gaelic are **eaglais** and **cladh** respectively), and is very common in placenames. These do not always mention a saint; Keills in Argyll is just 'cells', 'church', and Killin in Perthshire is 'white church'. Kilmarnock was known for its weaving industry; a Kilmarnock cowl or hood was a woollen night cap.

Kyle: thin; a narrow stretch of water. Gaelic **caol**. The word is very common in placenames but takes several different forms in English – **Kyle** (Lochalsh), **Col**intraive (Argyll), **Caol** (Lochaber), Balla**chul**ish (Loch Leven), **Kel**man Hill (Aberdeenshire), **Kil**churn (Loch Awe, Argyll), Eddra**chill**is (Sutherland). This is due to factors such as the fluidity of spelling in earlier centuries and the inadequacies of non-Gaelic-speaking scribes, as well as the fact that **caol** would have slightly different pronunciations throughout the Highlands. This is one of the origins of the surname (and now male forename) Kyle. The other is from the district of Kyle in Ayrshire, named after Coel, who ruled there about 400 A.D.

Kyloe: a type of small Highland cattle. Gaelic **Gaidhealach** 'Highland'. Cattle from the Highlands and Islands were a regular sight at lowland markets such as Falkirk.

L

Lachlan: Scandinavian. Gaelic **Lachlann**. A male forename. The meaning is (sea)loch land, **loch** being used in Gaelic for both fresh and sea water, and the reference is to the many fiords in Scandinavia.
Lochlann is the Gaelic for Scandinavia. The Vikings were, of course, well known in Scotland and at one time ruled large parts of the country. The clan MacLachlan (various spellings) were based in Cowal, at Strathlachlan, where the chief still lives, and there is a Kirklauchlane just south of Stranraer in Wigtownshire.

Lewisian: of Lewis, a geological term meaning pre-Cambrian. Lewis in Gaelic is **Leòdhas**, often referred to as **Eilean Leòdhais** 'The Isle of Lewis', of uncertain meaning, or **Eilean Fraoich** 'Heather Island', though it is not itself an island. The island has nothing to do with the name Lewis, which is of Germanic origin and found today in the forms Ludvig, Louis, and Ludovic.

Linn: a waterfall, a pool. Also lin. Gaelic **linne**. This is not the word for *waterfall* in modern Gaelic – **eas** is used instead – and in any case *linn,* 'waterfall' is from an old English word. But *linn* 'pool' is from Gaelic **linne**. The meaning extends from a pool at the foot of a waterfall to a much larger stretch of water; Loch Linnhe[29] at the foot of the Great Glen is based on this word, though in Gaelic it's **An Linne Dhubh** for the northern part and **An Linne Sheileach** for the southern part. So here **linne** is 'firth'; on the other side of the country the Firth of Tay is **An Linne Tatha**. Inland from the Firth of Tay the word appears in Lindores in Fife (unless it is the cognate Old British root found in modern Welsh *lynn*), and this is probably also the derivation of the various Lintons 'Farmstead by the Pool' in the Borders (also a surname); in England the reference is more likely to be to flax (lint) or a waterfall mentioned above. But Lincoln in England is 'The (Roman) Colony by the Pool' from the Old British form of **linn**, and the very common Latin *colonia*.

Loaghtan: an Isle of Man sheep with four horns and brown fleece. This is really a Manx word, but Manx is quite close to Gaelic. In Manx *loaghtyn* is brown (of sheep; also of a hare, *loaghtyn beg*). The literal meaning is mouse-brown, from Manx *lugh* (Gaelic **luch**) 'mouse' and *doan* (Gaelic **donn**) 'brown'. The sheep is called *keyrrey* (Gaelic **caora**) *loaghtyn*.

Loch: lake. Gaelic **loch**. The word is peculiar to Scotland and Ireland (where it is spelled *lough*), though it is, of course, cognate with English *lake*, Welsh *llwch*, French *lac*, Italian *lago* etc. There is even a modern Cornish form, *loh*, from a hypothetical earlier *logh*, which is found in the place-names Looe and Duloe in that part of what is now England. There are actually a few minor lakes in Scotland, some of them artificial, and even major ones could be called *lake* if circumstances required; *The*

---

[29] For the non-Gaelic spelling linnhe with inserted **h** see under **gillie**.

Lady of the Lake, for instance, refers to Loch Katrine, but Scott, with one eye on Arthurian legends and the other on an English readership, preferred the word *lake* in the title, though he uses *loch* at times within the poem. The often-quoted Lake of Menteith isn't a lake either; it's a corruption of the Laich of Menteith, *laich* being a Scots form of *low*. Used as a noun the word means low-lying ground, a plain, as in the Laich of Moray, the coastal strip stretching between Forres and Fochabers, and, in the form *laigh*, Laigh Kilmory (Kintyre), Laigh Fenwick (Ayrshire) etc. So the idea is *The loch on the low lying part of Menteith*, the Gaelic name for which is **Loch Innis MoCholmaig**, after a St Colman[30]. The island in the loch where the monks lived is anglicised as *Inchmahome*.

As mentioned under **Lachlan**, above, **loch** can mean a sea loch or a fresh water loch,

which accounts for Loch Uisg(e) in Mull ('fresh water loch'), so named to distinguish it from the sea lochs *Spelve* and *Buie* on either side of it. A great many towns and villages contain the word **loch** and it and *Lochhead* (a translation of *Kinloch*, from Gaelic **ceann** 'head') are also surnames.

A **lochan** is a small loch; masculine nouns use the suffix *-an* to express a diminutive, like Scots *-ie*; *laddie* (from *lad*) is Gaelic **balachan** (from **balach**).

Lochaber axe: a battle axe with a long wooden handle, often with a metal hook on the end. Gaelic **tuagh-chatha**. Lochaber, **Loch Abar**, is a district in Inverness-shire around Fort William, of disputed meaning; it is either 'muddy loch' (modern Gaelic **eabar**) or 'confluence loch' (the Pictish / Old British *abar* = Gaelic **inbhir**) mentioned above under Inverness, the confluence being that of the Rivers Lochy and Nevis into Loch Linnhe.

---

[30] There were over 200 saints with this name, which means dove (Latin columba; see under Malcolm), the most famous of whom was St Columba, **Calum Cille**, of Iona.

Logania: an Australian family of plants, named after James Logan, a 17th / 18th century botanist. A loganberry is named after a later Logan. The surname is Gaelic **Logain** or **Loganach**, meaning 'a hollow', and Logan is a village in Ayrshire near Cumnock. The usual placename form, however, is *Lagg* or the diminutive *Laggan* (also a surname), e.g. on the Caledonian Canal, retaining the vowel of Gaelic **lag**, though Gaelic does not allow a double **g**.

Lovat: a greyish-green wool, sometimes with yellow and blue tinges; cloth made from this. Gaelic **lobhta** is thought to be the source, meaning 'rotten, putrid, foul-smelling'. The reference would be to the placename Lovat at the west-end of the Beauly firth, with a possible allusion to decaying seaweed and other waste brought in on the tide. The modern Gaelic for Lovat is **A' Mhoroich**, the root of which is **muir** 'sea', and indicates land prone to flooding by the sea, which would suit **lobhta**. This was the territory of the clan Fraser, whose chiefs traditionally use in Gaelic the name Simon, Gaelic **Sìm**, and are known by the patronymic **Mac Shimidh**, from which comes the surname MacKimmie[31]. Other clan chiefs used similar patronymics, as, for instance, **Mac Cailein Mòr**, the Duke of Argyll, head of Clan Campbell.

Loy: a spade, shovel, with a footrest projecting from the shaft. Gaelic **laighe**. This is really an Irish word; J.M. Synge, in *The Playboy of the Western World*, describes its use as a weapon:

> I just riz (raised) the loy and let fall the edge of it on the ridge of his skull…

Lymphad: a West Highland galley, rather like a birlinn (see under **birlinn** above). Gaelic **long fhada** 'long ship'. **Long** is thought to be a borrowing from Latin (*navis*) *longa* 'long ship', i.e. warship, in which case **long fhada** is a

---

[31] For the disappearance of the **s** sound from a lenited **s** see under Hamish.

55

tautology, which often happens when one language uses a word which it does not understand from an earlier language. **Long** 'ship' appears in Longa Island (another tautology) in the Gairloch – ship island (Norse) + island (English) – and in Loch Long which is found twice (off the Clyde and off Lochalsh), though 'loch of ships' would seem to be a possible name for almost any sea loch. **Fada** 'long' occurs in Loch Fad in Bute and Ben Attow, **Beinn Fhada** in Kintail, the latter showing a silent lenited **f**, a normal feature of Gaelic.

M

Mac: son. Gaelic **mac**. Unlike English *son*, and the equivalent in many other languages (but not Icelandic), it is used only of males, the feminine equivalent being **nic**. So *MacDonald* can be a male or female surname in English, but in Gaelic it's **MacDhòmhnaill** and **NicDhòmhnaill** respectively. Another difference from English is that the word after **mac** changes to the genitive case in Gaelic. Donald MacDonald is fine in English, but in Gaelic it's **Dòmhnall MacDhòmhnaill**. So it is better to translate **mac** as *son*, rather than *son of*, since the *of* part appears in the genitive case; if **mac** meant *son of* there would, in theory, be no need to change the next word to the *of* form.

Mac is quite common in place-names, as MacDuff in Banff, Balmacara on Lochalsh etc. A few **mac** names have become established in English, describing inventions or characteristics of bearers of the name; so *macadam*, a type of road surface; *macadamia nut*, an edible Australian nut; *mac(k)intosh*, a waterproof coat; *Macmillanite*, a Presbyterian reformer; *McCarthyism*, persecution of suspected communists; *McNaughten rules*, rules regarding the defence of insanity in English law.

Machair: low lying pasture land by a sandy seashore. Gaelic **machair**. The name occurs in several placenames, as The Machars peninsula in Wigtownshire, and Machrins in Colonsay, and is a Gaelic equivalent of laich / laigh mentioned under **loch** above; the Laich of Moray is **Machair Mhoireibh. A' Mhachair(e) Ghallda** is also another way of describing the Lowlands of Scotland, in addition to **A' Ghalltachd** mentioned above under **Gallowglass**.

Màiri: a Gaelic form of *Mary*. Also Mairi. A female forename. The form *Mhairi* is also found, sometimes Anglicised as *Vari*, representing the Gaelic vocative case, but this is incorrect, as explained under **Hamish** above, and is bestowed as a forename by those who do not know Gaelic but who are sympathetic to the language.

Malcolm: servant of St Columba. A male forename and a surname. Gaelic **Calum**. The first part of the name is **maol** 'bald, tonsured', referring to the hairstyle of monks of the time, and occurs in the surnames MacMillan, **MacMhaolain** and **MacIlleMhaoil**, Malise, **Maol Ìosa,** as well as Irish

Malone and various surnames with *mul-* as *Mulholland* etc. It is a also found in placenames, as Amulree, **Àth Maol Ruibhe** in Perthshire and Ballochmyle, **Bealach Maol**, in Ayrshire, and, from Old British cognates, Melrose in the Borders, and Mellor and Malvern in England. See also under **muley** below. The second part of the name *Malcolm* is **calman** 'dove', from Latin *columbus* or *columba*, from which is also English *columbine* etc. The related surname MacCallum, **MacCaluim**, is normally, but erroneously, spelled with a double **l** in English, which may have given rise to the non-Gaelic spelling of the forename as *Callum*.

Mart: a cow fattened and slaughtered, then salted to provide food for the winter. Gaelic **mart** 'a cow'. The beast was usually killed around Martinmas (**An Fhèill Màrtainn**), the 11th November, but the long vowel on **Màrtainn** and short vowel on **mart** are rather against any etymological connection. Instead, the root is that found in **marbh** 'dead'; middle Irish had *martad* 'slaughter', from Latin *mors* 'death', English *mortal*. Rhynamarst, **Ruigh nam Mart** 'Hillside of the Cattle', some three miles south-east of Tomintoul shows the sibilant **r** commonly sounded in the combination **rt**.

Messan: a small dog, a lapdog. Gaelic **measan**. Burns, in *The Twa Dogs* says of one of them:

but wad hae spent an hour
caressin,
ev'n wi' a tinkler-gipsy's messin.

Mhairi: See under **Màiri** above.

Mod: a competitive Gaelic musical and literary festival held annually. Gaelic **mòd**. There are also local *mods* in addition to the main national *mod*. The word means *a meeting, court, assembly* and is cognate with English *moot*. It appears in Maud in Aberdeenshire, and in **Tom a' Mhòid**, a hillock in Dunoon where trials were held and judgements passed; the name is preserved in a nearby street. *Courthill*, **Cnoc a' Mhòid**, at Lunan Bay, Angus is similar. Since **mòd** is of

Norse origin it is not surprising to find it in several placenames in England, e.g. *Motcombe* 'a valley where meetings take place', though it is perhaps surprising that such an important Gaelic festival should have a non-Gaelic name.

Morag: big, great. Gaelic **Mòrag**. A female forename, a diminutive of the less common **Mòr**, of similar meaning. It is sometimes arbitrarily rendered as *Sarah* in English (see under **Fenella**, above).

Moravian: of Moray, an inhabitant of Moray. From the Latin form *Moravia* of Gaelic **Moireibh** 'Sea Settlement'. See also under **Murray**, above.

Mormaor: a provincial governor, a steward of Pictish provinces. Gaelic **mòrmhaor**. The word is made up of **mòr** 'great' and **maor** 'a steward'; modern Gaelic for the latter is simply **stiùbhard**, from the English, but **maor** is heard occasionally, for instance in **maor-cladaich** 'coastguard'. The word is from Latin *maior* 'greater', from which are also English *major* and *mayor*. It occurs in The Mearns, **A' Mhaoirn** (territory administered by a steward), another name for Kincardineshire, and is found also in Renfrewshire, better known in its *Newton* form. Surnames are Mearns and Mair, the latter an obsolete Scots word for a legal officer of the crown.

Muley: hornless, a cow without horns. Also mulley, mooly. Gaelic **maolag**. Scots has the forms *mulloch* and *moylie*. The root of the word is **maol** 'bald, bare, blunt', and so it is also used to mean a rounded hill, as Muldoanich, a small island to the south of Barra, and Glas Maol, a Munro, the highest peak in Angus. **Maol** is the Gaelic form of a old Celtic word; the Welsh is *moel*, from which, in the sense of *bald* many of the surnames *Moul(d)*, *Vowle*, *Fowles* (all with various spellings) derive; and the meaning *hill* appears in the English villages of Queen Camel and West Camel.

Mull: a promontory. Gaelic **maol**. This may be the same word as the preceding, but the sense is likely to have been influenced by old Norse *muli*, 'snout', and the Gaelic is probably a borrowing. The Vikings were of course very active around the headlands of the west coast and the islands, and *mulls* are found in Orkney and Shetland, where they can't be from Gaelic, since it was never spoken there. Nor does the word have this meaning in early Old British.[32] Gaelic was, of course, familiar with the use of facial features to describe the landscape; it uses **sròn** 'nose', and **gob** 'beak' to name promontories.

Mungo: blessed protector. A male forename. Gaelic **Mungan**. This was another name for Kentigern, a saint who lived in the 6th century and founded a church in Glasgow. Glasgow cathedral, originating in the 12th century, was dedicated to him. The origin of the word is, in modern Gaelic, **mo + fhionn**

---

[32] Modern Welsh for promontory is **penrhyn** or **pentir**, Gaelic **ceann** 'head' with **r(o)inn** 'point' and **tìr** 'land' respectively.

+ cù; **mo** is *my* (see also under **Kilmarnock** above), **fhionn** is used in its now obsolete sense of *blessed*,[33] and **cù** is *dog* in the sense of watchdog, protector. In theory the nasal mutation of Welsh would have produced something similar to Mungo but this can't be correct since it would mean that the stress was then on the possessive adjective **mo** (earlier Welsh *myn*), which was never the case.

Munro: a mountain of 3000 feet and over. The term originally referred to Scottish hills, of which there are 283 Munros at the last count, following the recent (2009) demotion of Sgùrr nan Ceannaichean in Ross and Cromarty, but is sometimes extended to the rest of Britain. Sir Hugh Thomas Munro (1856-1919), who first compiled a list, was born in London, but his father had an estate near Kirriemuir in Angus. The surname in Gaelic is **Rothach**, which has traditionally been connected with the River Roe in Londonderry, Northern Ireland. The prefix *mun* is a form of **bun** 'base', 'root', 'mouth of a river' due to nasalisation / eclipsis, as found also in Munlochy, **Bun Lòchaidh**, in the Black Isle.

Murdo: sea warrior. Gaelic **Murchadh**, also Anglicised as *Murdoch*. A male forename. The root is **muir** 'sea', as found in English *marine*, etc, and in other European languages. Other forms of the name are *Murchie, Murchison*, and the Irish *Murphy*. There is also a less common Gaelic form **Muireach**, also meaning *sailor*, though it has become confused with an obsolete word meaning *sovereign, lord*; *MacVurich* (showing **v** for lenited **m**, as normal; see also under **Màiri**) is from this word. The intrusive **d** in the English forms of the name appears in the placename *Lesmurdie*, a few miles south-west of Huntly, whereas

---

[33] **Fionn** now means *fair, white*, but its cognate Welsh *gwyn*, still means *blessed* (as well as white), and the areas in which St Mungo worked were Old British-speaking at the time. For other instances of the lost **f** sound of a lenited **f** see under **Atholl, Farquhar, Fergus, Finlay, Fail** and **Lymphad** above.

Pitmurchie in Aberdeenshire is more Gaelic (and Pictish).

Murlain: a round wooden basket with a small opening at the top. Also murlan, murlin. Gaelic **mùrlainn**, **mùrlach**, **mùrlag**. It is used by fishermen, but was also used on crofts for holding wool.

Murray: settlement by the sea. Gaelic **Moireach**. A male forename and a surname, from the north-east province / county now spelled *Moray*, Gaelic **Moireibh**. The root of the word is **muir** 'sea', as in **Murdo**, above.

N

Noggin: a small cup, usually of wood; a small drink. Gaelic **noigean**. The origin of this word is uncertain; the Gaelic *-an* at the end of the word (see above under **Aidan**, **bothan** etc) has the appearance of a diminutive, which would suit the meaning well, but English also has *-n* diminutives, as *cat / kitten*, and this too would suit, since *nog* in English is *a drink*; so

the word is likely to be of English origin.

O

O': grandchild, descendant. Gaelic **ogha**, Irish *Ó*. The Gaelic looks quite different from the Irish, but the gh doesn't really belong to the word and is there just to separate the syllables, since **oa** is not a Gaelic vowel combination. But the Gaelic is more like another earlier Irish form *ua*. There is no apostrophe in Irish *Ó* and the word is now usually written without an apostrophe in Anglicised forms of names, as O Brien, etc. The same is happening to English words in Scots, so that John o Groats is now an optional form.[34] Some Irish progenitors of *O-* names can be dated to the 10th century; Scottish clans began to emerge a couple of centuries later, and used, where appropriate, **mac** instead.

---

[34] Instances of Scots verse in this book use the traditional spelling, however, following the standard texts from which they are quoted.

Och: an interjection with various shades of meaning, as *annoyance, regret, surprise*, or a rather meaningless prefix, as *och well, if….* In Gaelic the word has the more restricted use of *alas* and is really onomatopoeic, imitative of a sigh; it's a shortened version of **ochòin**, discussed below under **ohone**.

Ogam: A Celtic alphabet of some twenty 'letters'. Also ogham. Gaelic **ogham**. These consisted of straight lines meeting or crossing another longer line, the latter usually the edge of a stone slab. It was invented in Ireland around the fourth century A.D., attributed to the legendary Celtic god Ogma, and came to Scotland a century later with the Irish colonisation of Dalriada. There are about 30 Ogam stones in Scotland but, although they can be transliterated into Roman script, they are unintelligible; they were presumably written in Pictish and most of them are found in what were Pictish areas.

Ohone: alas! Also ochone. Gaelic **ochòin**. Now a rather old-fashioned word; modern Gaelic is more often just **och** or **mo thruaighe**. When used in English it tends now to have a jocular effect.

Ollav: a doctor, a learned man. Also ollamh. Gaelic **ollamh**. The root of the word is the now obsolete **oll** 'great, grand'. In modern Gaelic it is generally used to mean 'professor'.

Oscar: a legendary Fingalian hero, whose name means 'champion, warrior'. Gaelic **Osgar**. A male forename. Given that this is the meaning, it points to the root of the word as **sgar** 'to split', referring to prowess with the sword. There is also the noun **osgar** 'champion' and the adjective **osgarach** 'intrepid', supposedly named after the Fingalian hero, but they are rarely found though they appear in Dwelly. Oscar was the son of Ossian, mentioned next.

Ossian: a legendary 3rd century warrior and poet, the son of Fingal. Gaelic **Oisean**. His name is the diminutive of **os**, an old word meaning 'elk', 'deer', probably a reference to his speed, and also to the fact that his mother, according to Gaelic legend, had been turned into a white hind by a malevolent magician. There are various places named after him, as Loch Ossian, just to the west of Loch Ericht in Inverness-shire, with the adjacent Strath Ossian, and Ossian's Cave in Glencoe. For the Ossianic ballads see under **Finn** above.

Oy: a grandchild. Also oye, oe. Gaelic **ogha**. See under **O'** above.

P

Partan: a small edible crab. Gaelic **partan**, **portan**. Since this word contains the letter **p** it is not an original Gaelic word; **p** was not in the original Gaelic alphabet and so words containing it, of which there are many, have been borrowed from other languages, mainly English, French and Latin. The origin of **partan** is not clear, however, unlike the case of Geocrab in Harris 'crab ravine' from Norse, but it appears in Lochportan in North Uist and Port nam Partan just north of Calgary bay in Mull. A connection with Latin *Parthicus* 'Parthian' has been suggested; Latin writers refer to Parthian leather dyed red. But the edible partan has a black shell, whereas the non-edible variety has a reddish shell.

Pellock: a porpoise. Also pellack, pellach. Gaelic **peileag**. As mentioned under the previous entry this is not an original Gaelic word, and is probably from the Scots *pellock*. More original Gaelic is **muc-bhiorach**, 'sharp-pointed pig'.[35] But the origin of the Scots word is unclear, and the letter **p** in a Gaelic word does not preclude borrowing by English or Scots, as **pibroch,** below, shows.

Pet: a tame animal. Gaelic **peata**. The letter **p** indicates, as ever, that Gaelic has borrowed this word, probably

---

[35] By analogy with **muc-mhara**, 'whale'.

from an Indo-European root meaning *to become accustomed to*. A connection with French *petit*, English *petty* is now discounted. English, in turn, seems to have borrowed the word from Gaelic / Irish; it appears in Old Irish, but is not attested in English until the 16th century.

Pibroch: the traditional classical music of the bagpipe, consisting of a theme or ground (**ùrlar**) with subsequent variations following an established pattern. See above under **ceòl mòr**, which is really the equivalent of *pibroch*; **pìobaireachd**, from which English *pibroch* was taken, simply means 'piping', including light music, jigs etc. The basis of the word is late Latin *pipa*, 'a pipe', a root found in other European languages, as French *pipe*, German *Pfeife* and so on. Yet these languages, and many others in Europe, have native words for the instrument, as *cornmeuse, Dudelsack*[36], unlike

Gaelic, even though **a' phìob mhòr** plays a vastly greater role in this country than do the European equivalents in their countries. Curious also is the fact that the word for a bagpipe reed, **ribheid**, is from the English; the other parts of the bagpipe, however, have Gaelic names.

Pillion: a cushion or saddle for a second rider on a horse, or behind the driver of a motorcycle etc; a pack saddle. Gaelic **pillean**. From Latin *pellis*, 'skin, hide', the origin also of Gaelic **peall**, of similar meaning.

Plaid: a long woollen cloth, usually tartan or checked, worn over the shoulder. It was, and still is in certain circumstances, a feature of Highland dress; a *plaid-man* was an old term for a Highlander. Gaelic **plaide** 'blanket'. A *plaid* in Gaelic is **breacan**, which also means *tartan*. The plaid was also used by Lowlanders, such as shepherds; Burns, in his poem *O wert thou in the cauld blast* continues

---

[36] with this German instrument compare Scots *doodle*, to play the bagpipe or other reed instrument, and see also **port-a-beul** below.

…my plaidie to the angry airt,
I'd shelter thee…

The pronunciation of *plaid* in England as *plad* is much closer to the Gaelic vowel sound. The word is usually regarded as borrowed from Latin *pellis*, mentioned in the previous entry, and again there is some doubt as to whether Gaelic influenced English (less likely), or vice versa (more likely). From *pellis* are also English *pelt*, *pellicle* and *pellagra*, the idea being a covering. But the verb *to ply*, i.e. *fold*, has also been suggested as a derivation.

Plouk: a small lump, a pimple. Also plook. Gaelic **pluc**. A word of disputed origin, but certainly not original Gaelic, as the **p** shows. It is possibly related to English *block*, Gaelic **ploc** 'a round lump', the genitive of which is **pluic**. But it may simply be from an old English dialect word *plowke* 'a growth, protuberance'. Plockton in Lochalsh is **Am Ploc** 'The Pimple', i.e. a lumpish headland.

Pollack: a sea fish of the same family as cod, haddock, whiting etc. Also pollock. Gaelic **pollag** can also mean *powan*, or *pollan*, the freshwater fish, also known as a lake herring, found in Loch Eck and Loch Lomond. The root of the word is **poll** 'pool', 'swamp' to which English *pool* is also related, as is the Pollok area of Glasgow and the surname Pollock.

Port: a tune, especially one played on the pipes. Gaelic **port**. Sir Walter Scott with his typical enthusiasm for things Gaelic used the word in *The Lay of the Last Minstrel*:

The pipe's shrill port aroused each clan.

The word is thought to be borrowed from Latin *portare* 'carry' – as in the phrase 'can't carry a tune' – with the related sense of 'catch'; a catch was a type of music, like a round, which developed in the 17th century, just before the pipes became widespread in the Highlands. There may also be the idea of the sound 'carrying'; compare Italian *portavoce* 'megaphone'. **Port-a-beul** is mouth music,

Scots *diddle*[37], singing without meaningful words to provide music for dancing in the absence of any instrument. **Beul** 'mouth' is the root of the word **Beurla** 'the English language', i.e. *mouthings, speech*. Beurla was also used to mean Scots, with a qualifying adjective such as **Albannach**; **Albais** is a modern term.

Pow: a slow-moving ditch of water, a marshy pool, a creek. Gaelic **poll** 'pool, mire'.

Powan: See under **pollack**, above.

Praiseach: a dish of porridge, sometimes with vegetables, as a kind of broth. In Gaelic, also **praiseach**, the word is used for varieties of kale, as befits its Latin origin *brassica*, as well as mustard, cress etc.

Ptarmigan: a type of hardy mountain grouse, a white grouse. Gaelic **tàrmagan**. The English spelling has a pseudo-learned addition of an initial **p**, as if giving the word a classical origin, like Greek initial *pt* found in words such as *Ptolemy, pterodactyl* etc. In the latter, *ptero* means 'wing', and is used in at least another dozen English words, a fact which may have influenced the English spelling of this Scottish bird. For the unnecessary insertion of **p** see also **Campbellite**, above. Initial **pt** is not a Gaelic combination, and so the reverse of the situation under discussion is found in the rarely heard **tiosan**, a drink made from water and oatmeal or barley, from English *ptisan* (perhaps following the alternative English spelling *tisane*).

The ptarmigan's plumage turns white in winter as camouflage amidst the snow. Tennyson in *The Last Tournament* describes how:

> The ptarmigan that whitens
>   ere his hour
> woos his own end.

Meall nan Tàrmachan is a Munro (see above) a few miles north of Killin, Perthshire.

---

[37] compare *doodle* above under **Pibroch**.

Puss: the face. See above under **buss**.

and can be seen from the ground.

Q

Quaich: a cup, bowl. Gaelic **cuach**. The word is cognate with Latin *caucus*, 'a cup', itself borrowed from Greek; it is very rare in both languages, and the fact that there is only one, very obscure, recorded instance of it in Latin argues against a borrowing.[38] It is probably from an Old English word *ceac*, itself borrowed from Byzantine Greek. The word is also used to mean a bowl-shaped hollow in a hill (see also **corrie**, above) and occurs in Anglicised placenames usually in the form *quoich*, as in Kinlochquoich, west of the Great Glen, and its associated glen, river and loch, and Duniquaich (various spellings) the hill overlooking Inveraray castle on Loch Fyne; a watchtower, built on the summit in 1748, still remains

R

Rath: a prehistoric circular hill fort, usually of earthwork. Gaelic **ràth**. The word is marked obsolete in Dwelly, and its modern equivalent would be **dùn**, (though this is usually stonework), but since hill forts are themselves obsolete one could say the same of the word **dùn**. **Ràth** seems to have been an earlier word, with a strong Irish flavour, and the fact that they occur together in Dounreay, **Dùnrath** rather suggests that the meaning of **ràth** had been forgotten and so **dùn** was prefixed to it as an explanation, something which happens all the time in placenames. Another instance is Dun Rahoy in Morvern, where Rahoy contains the element **ràth** (though the vitrified fort is actually on nearby **Tòrr an Fhamhair**). In general **ràth** is much less commonly used of existing hill forts in Scotland – **Beinn Ràtha** just south of Reay in Caithness is an

---

[38] **Cailis**, however, another word for cup, in the ecclesiastical sense of chalice, is a borrowing from Latin *calix*.

instance – but rather indicates where they used to be, whereas duns are quite visible, some well-preserved. There are quite a number of **ràth** placenames, as Raith[39] in Fife, and, in the form *roth*, Rothiemurchus near Aviemore; Rattray near Blairgowrie, Perthshire, is also a surname.

Reel: a lively Scottish dance; music for it. Gaelic **ruidhle**, **ridhle**. The origin of this word is not clear. If it is Gaelic, the root seems to be **ruith**, 'run, rush', contrasting it with the more sedate strathspey. But it may be borrowed from Scots *reel* meaning *whirl, swirl*. The term *reel* is first attested in the 16th century, earlier than its Gaelic form, which suggests an English / Scots origin, as does the fact that Gaelic has also borrowed **dannsa**, 'dance'. Reels come in various forms, two of them mentioned by Burns in *The Deil's awa wi' th' exciseman*:

There's threesome reels,
   there's foursome reels,
There's hornpipes and
   strathspeys, man…

Rolag: a roll of wool ready for spinning. Gaelic **ròlag** or **rolag**. The pronunciation of the word in English follows its spelling, i.e. doesn't end with a **k** sound as the Gaelic does. A borrowing from English *roll*, with the Gaelic diminutive feminine ending **-ag** found in Morag, Annag etc.

The Scots word is *rowins*; in the north-east a rowie is a small roll (of bread).

Rona: seal island. Gaelic **Ròna**. A female forename. The root is Gaelic **ròn** 'a seal' and Norse *ey* 'island'. Many islands off the west coast end in *-y* for this reason, but there is also a Gaelic version of this one, **Eilean nan Ròn** off the north coast of Sutherland. There are several islands called Rona, e.g. just north of Raasay, though for some the meaning is rather 'rough island'. The North Uist clan MacCodrum were known as **Sliochd nan Ròn**, people

---

[39] English instances of Raith, for instance Raithby, which occurs twice in Lincolnshire, have nothing to do with **ràth**, but are named after old Scandinavians.

of the seals because of an alleged descent from seal people.

Rory: red, ruddy. Gaelic **Ruairidh**. A male forname. It is often represented in English by Roderick, or Derick, for no good reason (see above under **Fenella**). Related surnames are Roy, MacGrory, MacCrorie, MacRury. The name occurs in Camusrory in Knoydart, and Inchrory, a few miles south of Tomintoul.

S

Sassenach: Saxon. Gaelic **Sasannach**. The word generally means an Englishman in both languages; the meaning *lowlander*, which it sometimes has in Scots, is not now found in Gaelic, which uses **Gall** instead. It is curious that the Celtic peoples call the English after the Saxons whereas the rest of Europe calls them after the Angles. This goes back a long way; Adamnan, the biographer of St Columba, writing before 700 A.D., refers to the Saxon inhabitants of the southeast of Scotland, who were surely Angles, and placenames

referring to the Saxons as Pennersaughs (earlier *-sax* and *-sex*), a few miles east of Dumfries, and Glen Sassunn at the south-east end of Loch Rannoch presumably relate to Angles. Many early chroniclers seem to have included the Angles and Jutes under the general term Saxon, which is slightly odd since the Angles were the more northerly settlers in England, East Anglia being further north than the Saxon regions of Es*sex*, Sus*sex*, Middle*sex* and Wes*sex*. The Welsh add to the confusion with their word for England, *Lloegr*, of uncertain origin. Saxon(e) as a surname is from English, and the name of the tribe is one of its meanings, but Sayce and Seys are from Welsh. Saxon was written *Sagsannach* in earlier Gaelic, where **gs** represents English **x** (or **ks**); neither **x** nor **k** appear in the Gaelic alphabet. The spelling **Sasannach** reflects the fact that **gs** is not a modern combination of letters in root words,[40] probably influenced

---

[40] Though it occurs in compounds, affixes, borrowings etc, as **tuigse** 'understanding', **bogsa** 'box'.

by Gaelic's traditional reduction of **x** (or **ks**) in Indo-European words to a simple **s** sound; Gaelic **os**, for instance, mentioned under **Ossian** above, is cognate with English *ox*.

Seannachie: an oral historian, one who can recite ancient lore, genealogies etc. Also seannachy, sennachie. Gaelic **seanachaidh**. They were patronised for centuries by clan chiefs, and after the break up of the old clan system after Culloden (1746), they found a more humble role in the **taigh-cèilidh** (see under **ceilidh**, above). Apart from their knowledge, their main asset was a prodigious memory. The root of the word is **sean** 'old', with which English *senile* is cognate, and which appears in several placenames, as Sanquhar, **Seann Chathair** 'Old Fortress' in the Borders, and Shannochie, **Sean Achaidh** 'Old Field' on the south coast of Arran. The surname Shand is thought also to be from **sean**, with the typically Scottish additional **d** (see under **Donald**, above). It and

Shannochie show the normal *sh* sound of Gaelic **s** with an **e** or **i**.

Seonaid: this is the Gaelic version of Janet, which itself is a diminutive of Jane. Gaelic **Seònaid**, which is also sometimes anglicised as Shona. A female forename. There is, of course, no letter **j** in the Gaelic alphabet, but the <u>sound</u> can be made with **d** followed by **e** or **i**. But with some forenames Gaelic uses **s** instead, as **Seasaidh** 'Jessie', **Seonag** 'Joan', **Seonaidh** 'Johnny', **Seòras** 'George', **Sìne** 'Jean' and so on. There was a fashion to transliterate George by **Deòrsa** around the time of the early Hanoverian kings of Britain but this has now fallen out of use. It was revived by the twentieth century poet George Campbell Hay, who used **Deòrsa** in the Gaelic form of his name.

Seumas: See under **Hamish**, above.

Shamrock: a trefoil, clover, the emblem of Ireland. Gaelic **seamrag**. This is a diminutive of the rarer (mainly Islay) form **seamair**. For the **-ag** feminine diminutive see under **Morag** above and for the sound of Gaelic **s** with a slender vowel (**e** or **i**) see under **Seannachie** above. The fact that the word trefoil means *three leaves* explains why four (and even five) leafed clover was so exceptional.

Shindig, **shindy**: See under **shinty**, below.

Shinty: A game like hurling / hurley or hockey, played with a stick (see above under **caman**) and ball by two teams of twelve players. Gaelic **iomain** or **camanachd**, the former having the sense of *driving forward* and the latter meaning *hitting with a club*. The word shinty is from **sìnteag**, 'a leap, a skip', itself from **sìn** 'stretch'. This is a feature of the game, particularly at the start and after each goal, when the ball is thrown high in the air by the referee, and a player from each side leaps to be the first to gain control of it. In other words shinty is the *leaping game*, just as curling is the *roaring game*, a term of some history; Burns

begins his poem *The Vision* with the lines:

The sun had clos'd the winter day,
the curlers quat their roaring play…

Shinty is also contrasted with that other great Scottish game, golf, which was also played with a **caman**; shinty is the leaping game as opposed to the more sedate golf. Originally it would have been referred to as **iomairt shìnteag** or similar, and the abbreviating to *shinty* might have obscured its origins; in the same way many, particularly in North America, may be unaware of the origin of the abbreviated term *soccer*.[41]

The boisterous nature of shinty is what lies behind the words *shindig and shindy*, a noisy commotion.

Sine: a Gaelic form of Jane or Jean, sometimes anglicised as Sheena. Gaelic **Sine**. A female

---

[41] It is, of course, a shortening of Association (football), so called to distinguish it from other types of football, as Gaelic, Rugby, American, Australian Rules etc.

forename. The form Sheena is close to the Gaelic sound of **s** with a slender vowel (**e** or **i**).

Skail: to scatter, disperse. Also scail, scale. The word has traditionally been connected with Gaelic **sgaoil**, of similar meaning but it is far from clear that there is any relationship between them.

Skelp: a slap. Gaelic **sgealp**. Another word whose origin has been disputed, but the Gaelic spelling with **p** indicates that it has been borrowed from English or Scots, and is probably onomatopoeic. Had it been an original Gaelic word it would have been written **sgealb** – an existing word meaning *splinter* – which would have a **p** sound at the end, but would be disyllabic in Gaelic pronunciation, which **sgealp** isn't.[42]

Skene: a dagger. Also skean. Gaelic **sgian** 'knife'. Skene-dhu, **sgian-dubh**

---

[42] Though **calpa** 'calf' (of the leg), for instance, is pronounced with three syllables.

'black knife' is the name given to the dagger tucked into a sock, an ornamental part of modern Highland dress. Skene-okkle, **sgian-achlais** 'oxter knife' is a dagger carried in the sleeve, and it is thought that the idea of placing the dagger in the sock arose from the desire of a friendly visitor to a house to remove it from its hiding place in his sleeve out of courtesy to his host.

The placenames Skene, an old castle and barony in Aberdeen-shire, and Scone in Perthshire, may, if their meaning of 'a split', 'chasm' is correct, be related to **sgian**. Powskein Burn, **Poll Sgine**, near Ericstane in Dumfries and Galloway, is apparently 'Pool of the Knife Slash' from its narrow appearance. There is a **Loch na h-Achlaise** on Rannoch moor.

Skye: a small long-haired, short-legged dog, of various colours – creamy white, fawn, grey, black. Also, more usually, Skye terrier; the breed was apparently developed in Skye in the 17th century. A well-known example was Greyfriars

Bobby, whose statue is at the top of Candlemaker Row, Edinburgh. Skye is from (**An t-Eilean**) **Sgìtheanach** or **Sgiathanach**, where the *-ach* ending makes the word an adjective to go with **An t-Eilean** (the island), meaning *indented* or *winged* respectively. Skye, the misty isle (**Eilean a' Cheò**) has a literary romance about its name; *over the sea to Skye* occurs as a phrase in H.E. Boulton's Skye Boat Song and again in R.L. Stevenson's *Songs of Travel*. An earlier ballad (Chevy Chase) has the lines:

> But I hae dreamed a dreary dream
> Beyond the Isle of Skye…

Slàinte: health. Gaelic **slàinte**. The word is used in English only as a toast to someone's health, often with **math** 'good'; **slàinte mhath** 'good health'. The adjective *healthy* is **slàn**, which is related to English *sal*utary, *sal*ubrious etc.

Slane: a spade for cutting and digging turf. Gaelic **sleaghan**. The root of this word is **sleagh** 'a spear', i.e. a pointed instrument, which is a fairly common Gaelic word, but the two diminutives **sleaghan** and **sleaghag** are more Irish, though Dwelly records the latter as being a Lewis word, in the sense of a sharp-pointed digging implement. Gaelic uses **treidhsgeir**, **tairsgeir** and similar for a peat spade.

Slew: a large amount. Also slue. Gaelic **sluagh** 'people', 'a multitude'. The word also has the specialised meaning of *fairy folk*; **Sìthean Sluaigh** 'the hill of the fairy folk', also known locally by the less romantic name *the camel's hump*, is near Strachur, Cowal. Glen Sloy **Gleann Sluaigh**, at the north-west side of Loch Lomond, reflects an alternative genitive form **slòigh**.

Slogan: a war cry; a catchword. Gaelic **sluagh-ghairm**. **Sluagh** 'people' (mentioned in the previous entry) and **gairm** 'a call', 'proclamation'. The idea is a rallying cry of the clans to war. Each clan had its own war cry, usually relating to a local topographical feature or a momentous deed from its history. The word was also spelled *slughorn*, which led some writers not acquainted with Gaelic to imagine that it was some kind of instrument like a horn. The 19th century poet Robert Browning wrote, in *Childe Roland to the Dark Tower came*:

Dauntless the slug-horn to
  my lips I set
and blew.

There are other earlier spellings, but the now established form *slogan* may have been coined by Sir Walter Scott; it was certainly popularised by him, as with many other Gaelic-related words.

Many readers will be familiar with *Gairm* as the name of a Gaelic publishing house and its iconic quarterly Gaelic magazine which was published from 1952 to 2002.

Slug: a gulp, a shot of whisky etc. Gaelic **slug** 'to swallow'.

Smidgen: a minute amount. Also smidgin, smidgeon. Gaelic **smid** 'word', 'syllable', 'sound' is possibly the origin. Scots has *smeech* 'a trace', 'a whisper' which is certainly from Gaelic, and reproduces the Gaelic soft **d**. The diminutive **smidean** is

rather unexpected – since **smid** is feminine, **smideag** would be usual – but this rule is not infallible.

Sonse; good fortune, luck. Also sonce. Gaelic **sonas** 'prosperity, happiness'. See also **donsie**, above. More common is the adjective *sonsie* 'comely, cheerful, hearty', well known from its use by Burns in *Address to a Haggis*:

Fair fa' your honest sonsie face
great chieftain o' the
  puddin-race!

Sorley: summer sailor, a Viking. Gaelic **Somhairle**, earlier Somerled, from Norse *Sumarliði*. Anglicised as Sorley. A male forename. Because of their small, by modern standards, boats, Vikings tended to raid during the summer months. An anonymous monk of the time tells in a poem, written in Old Irish, how he doesn't fear the imminent arrival of Vikings because the stormy winter weather will keep them away. *Sumarliði* was a fairly common Norse name, to judge from the various places in England featuring it, as Somer(s)by, and Somerleyton.

Sorn: to demand free lodging. The word, as well as the custom, is obsolete, from old Irish *sorthan*, and is first attested in the late 13th century.

Sowens: a dish of oat husks and meal steeped for some days in water, drained and boiled like porridge. Also sowans. Gaelic **sùghan**. The root of the word is **sùgh** 'juice'; English cognates are *suck* and *soak*. A more common modern Gaelic word is **làg(h)an**.

Spleuchan: a leather tobacco pouch. Gaelic **spliùc(h)an**. It is curious that Gaelic has a specific word for this without mentioning the word *tobacco*, and the presence of the letter **p** and the fact that tobacco would not have been known in the Highlands much before the 17th century suggests that the word has been borrowed. Welsh *blwch* 'a box', 'container' has been suggested, to which Gaelic has added an initial **s**; amongst other examples of this linguistic feature would be

sprèidh 'cattle', 'livestock', Welsh *praidd* 'a flock'.

Sporran: an ornamental pouch of varying sizes worn at the front of a kilt. Gaelic **sporan** 'a purse'. The word has been borrowed from Latin *bursa*, from which come also English *bursar, purse* etc. The addition of initial **s**, mentioned in the previous entry, is the more likely explanation for the Gaelic form rather than simple metathesis.[43] The surname MacSporran is sometimes anglicised to / translated by Purcell; they are a MacDonald sept and were treasurers to the Lords of the Isles.

Spreagh: cattle as booty, a raid, plunder. Also spreaghery, sprechery. The word is from **sprèidh** 'cattle', itself from Latin *praeda* 'booty'. Gaelic has added an initial **s**, as mentioned in the two previous entries; English cognates *predator* etc, haven't, though this is a device found elsewhere in English as *(s)lash, (s)quash* etc.

---

[43] Letters changing place within a word, as Gaelic **susbaint**, English *substance*.

Sprèidh itself doesn't mean *plunder*, the usual word being **creach**. Cattle raids were a regular feature of the Celtic lifestyle and go back a long way. The Irish epic *Táin Bó Cuálgne* 'The Cattle Raid of Cooley' describes an event in the first century A.D.

Spunk: a spark, mettle, a match, tinder. Gaelic **spong** 'a sponge'. Both this and English *sponge* are from Latin *spongia*, with the extended meaning of sponge-like substance, fungus, which was used to make tinder. Latin *fungus* was originally *sfungus* and is related to *spongia*.

Strath: a wide valley. Gaelic **srath**. The idea is *spread out*, the same root as **sràid** 'street' as well English *street*. The word is very common in placenames, as Strathmore, Strathspey etc.

Strontium: a whitish metallic element used in fireworks etc, and in its crystal form known as strontianite. Named after the village of Strontian in Sunart, **Sròn an t-Sìthein** 'The Promontory of the Fairy Hill' (see also under **banshee**, above) where strontianite was first discovered in 1790. The English version of the place name doesn't reproduce the Gaelic pronunciation; as the accent shows, the **ì** of **Sròn an t-Sìthein** is a long stressed vowel.

Other placenames with **sròn** 'nose', hence 'point, promontory' include Strone in Cowal, Argyll, and elsewhere. The surname Stronach, well-known in the person of **Mac an t-Srònaich** (Alexander Stronach) an outlaw and bogeyman of the 19th century, mainly on Lewis, is probably descriptive (having a remarkable nose) rather than a location name.

T

Taghairm: divination, summons, a method of foretelling the future. Gaelic **taghairm**. The root of the word is **gairm** 'call, invoke'. See also under **slogan**, above.

Taisch: a ghost, apparition; second sight. Also taish. Gaelic **taibhse**. Given the prominence of ghosts, fairies etc in Gaelic life and folklore it is not surprising that the Gaelic words for them have infiltrated English and Scots.

Tam o Shanter: a flat round woollen cap, usually with a toorie or pompom on top. Also tammy. The Gaelic element is *shanter*, thought to be **seann taigh** 'old house', or **seann tìr** 'old land'. See also under **Seannachie** above. As for Tam, a Scots form of Tom, the **a** vowel is retained in the surname MacTavish, the Gaelic form of which, **MacTàmhais**, makes the connection with Tam clearer, and illustrates the sounds of a lenited **m** (=v) and **s** with a slender vowel (=sh).

Tanist: the designated heir to a chieftainship or kingship. Gaelic **tànaiste**. Under the system of tanistry the heir (always male) was chosen while the present ruler was still alive, from extended family members. This was sometimes the ruler's brother, or the son of a previous ruler. The idea was to avoid succession disputes and to ensure that the whole tribe accepted the tanist. This system was used by Scottish kings up to the 12th century. Thus Kenneth I MacAlpine was succeeded by his brother Donald I, who was succeeded in turn by Constantine I, the son of Kenneth I. Later, Macbeth was succeeded briefly by Lulach, the son of his first wife, then by Malcolm III (Canmore), the son of Duncan I. A modern reference is found today in the Irish Republic, where the deputy prime-minister is known as the *tanaiste*.

Teuchter: a disparaging term used by Lowland Scots for a Highlander or Gaelic-speaker. This is quite a recent coinage (20th century), but its etymology is unclear. It is not itself a Gaelic word but seems to be vaguely onomatopoeic, supposedly representing the sort of sound frequently heard from a Gaelic-speaker. It's rather like the original meaning of *barbarian*, 'stammering', 'speaking unintelligibly', which Greeks of old used to describe foreigners, the word then extending to mean *foreign, non-Greek*. Similar

instances from speech habits in
English and Scots would be
Hooray Henry (sometimes shortened to *Hooray*), a loud, upper-
class rather philistine male, and
nyaff, a small, useless and
insignificant person, from the
earlier use of *nyaff* meaning to
talk in a senseless or frivolous
way, particularly by children.
The suffix -*er* may imitate the
Gaelic suffix -*air* / -*ear*, as in
clàrsair 'harper', **saighdear**
'soldier' etc.

Tinchel: a circle of hunters
surrounding and closing in on
trapped deer. Gaelic
timcheall 'around, about'.

Tir nan Og: The Celtic land of
the Blessed, the land of eternal
youth. Gaelic **Tìr nan Òg**
'Land of the Young'. This was
a mythical island far out in the
ocean to the west, sometimes a
land beneath the waves. **Tìr**,
which is cognate with English
*terr*ain, *terr*itory etc, occurs in
placenames such as Tiree and
Kintyre, **Cinn Tìre**
'Headland'. For **òg** see under
Gallowglass.

Tocher: a dowry. Gaelic
tochradh, **tochar**, the latter
being more Irish. Robert
Burns's poem *A Lass wi' a
Tocher* stresses the benefits of a
dowry. The surname Tocher,
fairly common in the north-
east, is, however, from another
tochar, an old word for *a
causeway*, as is the placename
Duntocher. Tocher is well
known in Scottish literary
circles as the title of the journal
of the School of Scottish
Studies, a magazine which
transmits the rich inheritance
of the country's oral traditions
in music, story etc in English,
Scots and Gaelic.

Toiseach: historically, a Celtic
leader, a thane, a clan chief.
Also toisech. Gaelic **toiseach**,
which in modern Gaelic means
beginning, leading. The word
occurs in Ireland in the form
taoiseach, the title of the Irish
Prime Minister. Surnames are
MacIntosh **Mac an Tòisich**,
Tosh and Toshack.

Tonnag: a shawl worn by
women. Gaelic **tonnag**. From
Latin *tunica*, as is English *tunic*.

Torquil: See under **Corrie**, above.

Torridonian: a geological term for pre-Cambrian rocks found in the north-west. From Torridon, **Toirbheartan**, a loch and village in Wester Ross. The derivation is uncertain; one possibility, as the Gaelic form suggests, may be from **tairbeart** 'isthmus', though it would not be a very narrow isthmus. But not all *tarberts* were narrow; Glen Tarbert in Morvern, between Loch Linnhe and Loch Sunart is almost as long as a direct route between upper Loch Torridon and Loch Carron.

Trews: tartan trousers. Gaelic **triubhas**, where the lenited **b** is pronounced like English **w**, as is often the case. Earlier versions of these also covered the feet. It is not certain whether Gaelic or Scots is the borrower. The letter **b** in the Gaelic is from Old Irish and Old French and suggests that Scots borrowed the word from Gaelic. If Gaelic had borrowed from Scots the **b** would need explaining, and although a lenited consonant is sometimes

inserted in a word borrowed from other languages to separate syllables, it is not usually **b**, and in any case the word could have been written *triùs* or similar. *Trews* is related to *trouse*, now *trousers*. **Seann Triubhas** 'Old Trews' is a well-known solo dance, sometimes anglicised as *Shantrews*.

Tuath: the people, peasantry. Gaelic **tuath**. The idea is *the masses*, and the word is cognate with English *tot*al, and ultimately with Teuton, Deutch, Dutch, meaning *people, nation*. There is a saying:

> **Is treasa tuath**
> **na tighearna.**
> The peasantry are stronger
> than the laird.

Tulchan: a stuffed calfskin placed beside a cow as an inducement to give milk. Gaelic **tul(a)chan** 'little mound, hillock', a diminutive of **tulach** (see under **Hoolachan**, above). Tulchan occurs in several placenames, as Glentulchan, a few miles west of Perth. A tulchan bishop was a 'bishop' created by the

Regent Morton after the Reformation, whose job was to 'milk' a diocese to enrich the local nobility.

Turlough: a lochan or boggy ground which dries up in summer. Gaelic **turloch**. This is thought to be the meaning of Glen Turret off Glen Roy east of Spean Bridge, and again just north of Crieff, Perthshire. The root is **tur** 'dry' (as in dry bread), more commonly found in **turadh** 'dry weather'. More usual Gaelic for *dry* is **tioram**, widely known from Castle Tioram[44] in Moidart. The Irish forename Turlough has nothing to do with *dry* but refers to the Norse god Thor.

Twig: to understand. A colloquial word thought to be from Gaelic **tuig** 'understand'. The word is first recorded in the 18th century, but *twig* in Scots means *a glance, glimpse* from earlier colloquial English *twig* 'to watch', i.e. 'to see' which is another way of saying *under-*

stand, so this may also be a factor.

U

Usquebaugh: an old name for whisky. Burns uses it in Tam o Shanter:

Wi' tippenny we fear nae evil;
Wi' usquabae we'll face the devil.

Gaelic **uisge-beatha** 'water of life', aquavit. **Beatha** is found in the surnames MacBe(a)th, MacBean, MacBain, and with the **b** lenited, MacVeigh (various spellings), and also in the female forename **Beathag**. The hereditary medical family of Beaton, who worked mainly on Mull and Islay in the Middle Ages, were really MacBeths. St Beathan features in several placenames, as Kirkbean, about 10 miles south of Dumfries.

W

Weem: an underground dwelling, a souterrain. From old Gaelic **ua(i)m**, 'cave',

---

[44] So-called because it was difficult to reach at high tide.

borrowed when the **m** was unlenited. The modern word is **ua(i)mh**. Hence Wemyss Bay In Ayrshire, Pittenweem in Fife, and the surname Wemyss. The more Gaelic form is found in **Loch nan Uamh** in Morar, the scene of the departure from Scotland by Prince Charles Edward Stuart in 1746 after the failure of the 1745 campaign, and Belnahua **Beul na h-Uamha** 'The Mouth of the Cave', a small slate island to the west of Luing.

Whisky: a distilled spirit. This is a shortened form of **uisge-beatha** mentioned above under **usquebaugh**. In this country it means Scotch whisky, though whisk(e)y is also made in Ireland, the USA, Canada, Japan, India, Brazil, South Africa and elsewhere.